The Good System

Patrick Henz

DEDICATION

To the Dots.

CONTENTS

ACKNOWLEDGMENTS

The book is based on W. Edwards Deming's famous concept "The System of Profound Knowledge". Although he conceived it before the internet, or even Artificial Intelligence, became popular, the idea anticipated intelligent algorithms, and the efficient collaborated between Human and AI.

1 THE GOOD SYSTEM

1.1 Welcome to the System

MIT professor W. Edwards Deming, statistician and business consultant published in 1993 his book "The New Economics for Industry, Governance, Education", where he explains the "System of Profound Knowledge".[1] This holistic concept had been a logical conclusion of his career.

In 1947 he encountered the Japanese culture, as the US Department of Army asked him to plan the later Japanese Census. He stayed in contact with the country to support with the reconstruction efforts. In his famous lecture to Japanese management in 1950 he pointed out that with improving quality as consequence expenses decrease and productivity & market share increase.[2] Before he could come to his conclusion, he had not only studied manufacturing and statistics, but also achieved a deep understanding of the local culture and actual situation. Due to this, he had been aware that the country not only had a high number of qualified workforces, but also that they already developed knowledge of the mater. He understood his task to push them further into the right direction and implement this knowledge:

---

[1] Deming, W. Edwards (1993): "The New Economics for Industry, Governance, Education"

[2] Deming, W. Edwards (1950): "Lecture to Japanese Management"

"In modern Japan many technicians, mathematicians, and statisticians are researching statistical product quality administration. Furthermore, since coming to Japan I have learned that the splendid achievement these people have made in statistical product quality administration is already apparent."[3]

Deming always stayed connected with the county, what should be in mutual benefit, as clearly the Japanese culture also influenced his later theories and publications, including his famous "System of Profound Knowledge".[4] Here he connected the understanding and appreciation of a system together with the philosophical theory of knowledge and psychology. In opposite to the early ages of automation, Deming included that the employee is not only inside the system, he defined him/her as a key part of it. A sign of respect for humanity itself. This philosophy is aligned with the Japanese Shinto-religion, which understands the human as part of nature and environment.[5] Based on Shinto, the Japanese culture developed the idea of "chowa" (Japanese for "a spirit of harmonious partnership"). In a connected world each action leads to a counter-action and similar to the "butterfly-effect" has numerous consequences.[6] To ensure sustainable and responsible growth, it is imperative to create win-win-situations between the directly involved partners, including to consider the benefit of other potential

---

[3] Deming, W. Edwards (1950): "Lecture to Japanese Management"

[4] Deming, W. Edwards (1986): "Out of the Crisis"

[5] Ito, Joi (2018): "Why Westerners fear Robots and the Japanese do not"

[6] Omiya, Hideaki (2018): "Chowa: A Business Philosophy to Bridge a Fractured World"

stakeholders, which do not have a voice or "seat the table".

The idea of Shinto is also to be found inside James Lovelock's Gaia theory. Here the British futurist and consultant to the NASA defined that a whole planet is similar to one living organism, meaning that all creatures as animals, plants and humans are part of one holistic organism.[7] Changes in the different populations influence the development of the whole planet. Based on this, changes easily could bring the established system out of its equilibrium, and doom all life.

The System of Profound Knowledge is a consequent development based on Deming's understanding that an organization is nothing more and nothing less than a sophisticated system. This idea he already lectured in the 1950s in Japan and later included in his book "Out of the

---

[7] Lovelock, James (1972): "Gaia as seen through the atmosphere"

Crisis". The company is a connected system, from procurement, over production to distribution. Important, it is not a closed system, but connects via various dots to the outside world. Not only via procurement or sales, but also production, human resources, management, etc. With this, Deming left the typical understanding of a win-win-situation, but wanted to teach the need for a sustainable long-term solution, so that all shareholders gain, including clients, management, employees, and society.[8]

As Deming defined his "System of Profound Knowledge", a broader exchange of data was still fiction. The name already underlines that a corporate system does not connect one brain with the different parts of the organizations, but includes the knowledge directly in all parts of the system. All connected employees include a part of the corporate knowledge. They are connected to data, information, knowledge and even wisdom. This via sensors, algorithms and other humans. Even if knowledge is available in all parts, based on requirements, the system can develop different global and local hubs to accumulate knowledge. Like an octopus, which not only has three hearts, but nine brains. Such structures support the perfect fit of the company to its ecosystem and can be temporary created. Aligned with the Gaia-Theory, the corporate system is not defined by borders, but features permeable membranes interictally connecting to clients, providers, business partners, influencers, neighbors and total society. Doing so, the system is in a continuous change, so less a construct made of steel and brick, but of liquid connections.

---

[8] Hunter, John (2012): "Appreciation for a System"

A company is a decentralized structure. Significant knowledge is at the top, but experience and intelligence are spread over the complete organizational infrastructure inside the individual employees. Astrophysicist Neil deGrasse Tyson explained that a planet does not technically orbits it host star, but instead both bodies effectively orbit their common center of mass.[9] This picture explains that all employees are responsible for their radius. Business consultant Ira Chaleff concludes that leadership is not about followers, and team-members do not exist to satisfy their leader. Instead both are part of the system and responsible for their area of gravity, this to maximize the efficiency of the complete system. As micro-system, the group has not only to fulfill its tasks, but also to uphold the company's vision and values. The same applies also for the single employee. To achieve this, all employees require at least a basic knowledge about the company's strategy and business philosophy. This comparison with astrophysics lets to the conclusion that each dot (employee, corporate values, Code of Conduct, processes, tools, etc., but also external ones likes providers, clients, society) has the power to influence, and due to this change the internal and external connections of the system, including the distance between the single dots.

Enzo Ferrari analyzed his business success: *"Factories are made of people, machines and bricks. Ferrari is made mostly of people."* A modern approach, especially in times of Industry 4.0. Business consultant and MIT-professor MIT professor W. Edwards Deming confirmed the employee's key-position

---

[9] deGrasse Tyson, Neil (2017): "Astrophysics for People in a Hurry"

with the four pillars of his "System of Profound Knowledge":

- Appreciation for a system
- Knowledge about variation
- Theory of knowledge
- Psychology[10]

This approach is based on his diverse background as engineer, statistician and management consultant. Important is that all four points interact with each other and so the sorted mathematical world of the system stands in direct contact with the philosophical knowledge ("Epistemology") and human psychology.

---

[10] Deming, William Edwards (1993): "The New Economics for Industry, Governance, Education"

The foundation is the system, planned by Deming from the supplier via the production assembly up to the consumer. Thanks to the detailed knowledge about systems and all factors that can influence them, we are able to plan and manage it as efficient as possible. Including information and experience, changes inside the process are not randomized, but are based on a theory (where the change should take place, what it would provoke and how it would affect the total efficiency) and get measured. To do so, it is not only necessary to predict the output of the potential change, but have a complete overview, which changes are available to execute.

The first two pillars are mathematically based and could be interpreted as a dehumanization of the working environment. To avoid such effect, Deming added philosophy and psychology as third and fourth pillars. This not only to underline the essential importance of the human factor, but also, he defined that all the four pillars had the same importance and due to this, only their holistic connection ensures sustainable success. *"They interact with each other. A change in on part cause changes in other parts."*[11][12]

---

[11] Canard, Frédéric (2011): "W.E. Deming, Pragmatism and sustainability"

[12] Henz, Patrick (2019): "Tomorrow's Business Ethics – Philip K. Dick vs. W. Edwards Deming"

1.2 Appreciation for the System

1.2.1   Poems

When Deming defined his System of Profound Knowledge, a broader exchange of data was still fiction. In 1993, the internet was already an established network, but due to a lacking graphical interface, most users had been students and professors. The same year, this was about to change with the release of the Mosaic Web Browser developed by the National Center for Supercomputing Applications at the University of Illinois at Urbana-Champaign. As the application was free for non-commercial use, it brought new groups to the internet, especially to the world wide web. Later, Mosaic lost ground against Netscape's 1995 Navigator, and its development was officially discontinued in 1997. Nevertheless, part of the browser survived, as Microsoft licensed it to use it as base for its Internet Explorer.

On December 20 of the same year, W. Edwards Deming died in age of 93. We only can assume how he would have updated his concept of a system to keep it aligned with network technology, sensors and more powerful hardware.

As expressed by the title, Deming did not understand the system as a pure connection of different players (departments inside a company) for the exchange of information, but the system itself including the knowledge.

Albert Einstein once said: "Information is not knowledge." Knowledge requires the logical interpretation of information. This often cannot be done at once, but requires a certain time, including for analyzing and reflection. The organizational structures are not the result of a natural process, but include human ideas and vision.

The poet, publisher and playwright Thomas Stearns Eliot asked in the words of the play "The Rock":

"Where is the wisdom that we have lost in knowledge?

Where is the knowledge that we have lost in information?"[13]

It can be understood as a homage to Eliot that more than half a decade later, the organizational theorist and consultant Russell L. Ackoff started his ideas regarding "From Data to Wisdom" with a poem:

"An ounce of information is worth a pound of data.

An ounce of knowledge is worth a pound of information.

An ounce of understanding is worth a pound of knowledge."[14]

The result became his pyramid consisting of four layers: data, information, knowledge, and wisdom. Ackoff already considered automation, and explained that *"wisdom deals with values"* and that it *"includes the exercise of judgement."* Nevertheless, it would be possible to phrase this in

---

[13] Eliot, Thomas Stearns (1934): The Rock

[14] Ackoff, Russell Lincoln (1989): "From Data to Wisdom"

algorithms, so that machines could automate related actions. On this other hand, it underlines that Artificial Intelligence can include wisdom, but such requires the manual input of humans. Machine Learning can detect statistical patterns and based on this knowledge, accordingly predict future scenarios, but it cannot act based on wisdom. Data, information and knowledge are manifestations of the past, in opposite to wisdom, what means the understanding of past, present and future. Ackoff defined knowledge as *"answers to how-to questions"*. Computer scientist Jennifer Rowley aligned knowledge with "decision support systems" and wisdom with "expert systems".[15] This leads to the question if Deming would had predicted such expert systems, would he had updated his concept to a "System of Profound Wisdom"? Maybe not, as even in the near future, a system cannot ensure wisdom on all levels of the corporation.

1.2.2 The Founder

We can assume that an entrepreneur and founder has neither a book of internal norms & regulations, nor a written Code of Conduct with defined corporate values. In the beginning exist only a handful of employees, so such documents are not necessary. Everyone has direct contact with top-management, and understands what they expect from the employees. With business success, rising workload and number of employees, there is no time anymore to

---

[15] Rowley, Jennifer (2007): "The wisdom hierarchy: representations of the DIKW hierarchy"

explain each employee what to do, so it becomes necessary to elaborate work-manuals. Strict labor-laws and unions furthermore require defined workers' rights and requirements, tax laws require to establish efficient accounting, and so on. To ensure that everybody knows and follows the founder's vision, it is imperative to define his / her values as corporate values. The company's Code of Conduct defines the various norms and expected behavior. All other internal regulations base on the CoC.

The various documents relate to the founder and represent his / her values, attitudes, experience and knowledge. Despite the founder, each employee shapes the organization. Key-employees are responsible to define new corporate regulations, processes, routines, and norms, even may update the Code of Conduct from time to time. All updates cause changes to the corporate system. Similar to the human backbone, the knowledge of former employees stays subconsciously active inside the company. If we analyze an organization as a system, we can add a third dimension to it, as today's structures and connections are shaped by internal and external events of the past, including that like the Big Bang, the company's founder acts as anchor for today's visible organization.

As the system is based on knowledge, it does not autonomously adapt to changes inside the ecosystem. A system purely based on information could be compared to the Blob from the movie with the same name. Here a gelatin like organism crashed on Earth and started to grow and consume living organism. Without higher intelligence and its only purpose to grow it just acted based on its sensors reacting to the surrounding.[16]

A knowledgeable system is structured to fulfil today and tomorrow the organizational purpose. In times of Digital Transformation and potential disruption of the actual business, management must have a concrete vision of the near future: digital maturity. As the destination is clear, there must be a plan to reach it. The execution of the plan needs a change of the system. Due to this, the actual setup is not optimized on the actual ecosystem, but a mixture of the actual optimum with the one expected tomorrow. Tue to this, Deming's system not only has its anchor in the past, but also connects to a fixed point in the future.

The connections are not limited to the department-level, but go further down. Each employee connects with internal and external actors. Furthermore, employees get connected

---

[16] Yeaworth, Irvin (1958): "The Blob"

with physical objects as work-places, computers, equipment, and non-physical objects, such as process, regulations, values, norms and attitudes. This reaches back so that the actual organization connects with the founder's original values, attitudes and vision. Bigger organizations have often an archive or even museum to collect and document such information. Pieces (including final products) relate to business decisions, but also private life.[17] Important is to support an objective research, for example collaborating with external historians, as with the distance of time, the perception of historical figures through actual glasses may lead to misinterpretations. In such cases, organizations are tempted to change the historiography to let founder and company shine in a more positive light. The author George Orwell described in "Nineteen Eighty-Four": *"Who controls the past controls the future. Who controls the present controls the past."*[18]

The efficient connection of the presence with the past and the future supports the organization protecting itself against corruption and fostering a sustainability strategy.

This is imperative, as corruption erodes the system. If projects get won with a bribe, instead of a combination of price and quality, it sends wrong signals to the Operations department, which underestimates the need to improve quality. Corruption could enter an organization from all different sides, for example, sales, procurement, project

---

[17] Henz, Patrick (2019): "Business Philosophy according to Enzo Ferrari"

[18] Orwell, George (1949): "Nineteen Eighty-Four"

management, but also HR. Management must ensure the proper maintenance of the system, done by Governance, Audit, Compliance or any other department.

1.2.3 The Idea

"An idea is like a virus, resilient, highly contagious. The smallest seed of an idea can grow." Dominick Cobb explains in the movie "Inception" the concept to create a virtual dream to manipulate individuals and extract restricted information from them.[19]

Professional hackers are firm believers of system-thinking. As today's cybersecurity offers bold protection, they detected a potential week point in the line of defense: the employee. Humans are connected with the company's IT system, and with the interaction ensure efficient and effective protection. This works if employees work based on corporate rules. Cognitive attacks aim to manipulate the perception of people exploiting their psychological vulnerabilities to let them perform actions and / or divulging restricted information. Using the antique concept of the wooden horse, hackers connect with the employee via email or phone-call to confront them with a constructed reality to let them act based on this perception. The unsuspecting employee lets the horse inside his / her head, not seeing that this is not a precious gift, but an army of soldiers.

---

[19] Nolan, Christopher (2010): "Inception"

Perception is based on the individual's experience, due to this, manipulation needs preparation. Social media is a relevant source of information. Bots autonomously "crawl" (due to this, this software is also known as "crawlers") through professional pages like LinkedIn. Doing so, the connected AI is not only able to understand the background of the individual, including position, education, etc., but also connect this information with other profiles. Like reverse engineering, the AI can elaborate an organizational chart, so that hackers understand who colleagues are, who is the direct manager and who is top-management. Precious information, for a personalized phishing email or call.

German business coach Tom Senninger developed in 2000 the Learning Zone Model, where the individual is most of the time in its personal Comfort Zone. For personal growth it is required to leave this state and enter the Learning Zone to seek new experiences. The individual could motivate itself for this, or react to external stimuli. If the self- or external-motivation gets too high, the effect becomes contra-productive, as the individual reaches the Panic Zone.[20]

According to this concept, hackers often try to push employees into the Panic Zone. Based on the "Stanley Milgram Experiment", the criminal takes advantage of psychological pressures, and requests the employee's support, even if this would mean bypassing of internal guidelines or external laws, like making a transfer to another bank account as originally agreed on. The interaction with a person who stands on potential higher level in the business relation means stress.[21] To foster this effect, such a phishing email could take advantage of other known stress situations. For example, the hacker would send it out at the end-of-year of the company or the tax-return season.

The hacker also can use an opposite tactic and present him or herself as in a weak situation to create pity. Important is to create a realistic picture inside the head of victim.

The created stories are taken from real-life scenarios, so that the victim feels empathy, as he or she already had been in such a situation or can imagine to be one day. Therefore, the person is willing to bypass internal security processes and may give out even confidential information. Important is that the hacker has the capability to keep up the vivid

---

[20] Henz, Patrick (2020): "Compliance Tales & Travels"

[21] Milgram, Stanley (1963): "Behavioral Study of Obedience"

picture in the head of the recipient. Due to this, such attacks are mostly done by telephone, known as social engineering.

The contact with a potential victim leads to higher level of stress for the employees, as they feel the pain and, as human, want to help, what often would lead to a deviation of corporate guidelines. As individuals feel the pressure to leave the uncomfortable situation as soon as possible, they may choose to bypass regulations, especially if they do perceive these guidelines as bureaucratic and non-efficient. Hackers are knowledgeable about these human vulnerabilities. A vivid example is the call of a female social engineer, pretending to be a young mother, using the sound of a crying baby in the background (easily to be found in YouTube), begging the call-center assistant to tell her the password of her potential husband.

This imagination works like an app or a computer virus inside the brain and let us execute behaviors, which are against our own interests. Already a short time after we answered to such a call, the power of this "virus" weakens and the individual receives his or her first doubts and starts to regret the actions.

The knowledgeable system is aware of the vulnerabilities of its human dots. Accordingly, it may not reduce the risk to zero, but nevertheless formalize the defense mechanism:

- Empower employees so that they are aware of their responsibilities, and perceive accountability.
- Especially in the state of panic, employees need clear messages, including easy to follow processes.

- The four-eyes-principle reduces the risk as, more employees would have to be affected by the virus. On the other hand, too many approval levels may lead to the bystander effect, taking away responsibility form the single employee. Also expressed by Deming: *"Divided responsibility means that no one is responsible."*

- A positive corporate culture with accessible management reduces the risk that employees are afraid to ask higher levels, when in doubt if a message is faked or not.

- Intelligent algorithms can automatically flag suspicious emails so that the employee gets aware of a potentially dangerous situation.

- Raising awareness is one of the most effective protections, regular workshops using real life-examples can support, but must be regularly repeated, as employees may forget about their individual vulnerabilities.

- Access to information and tools should be limited to the "need-to-know"- or "need-to-access"-principle. Such connections could be aligned with the idea of the zero-trust network. Employees which have access to sensible information should be object of regular background checks.

Of course, psychological manipulation could be combined or replaced with classic mafia methods. Also here, preparation is key to identify a potential vulnerable employee (as dot of the corporate system) to bribe this person, and if needed, combine this strategy with extortion. For example, an employee may be in financial problems.

Attackers offer money to help in critical situations. If the employee should resist, based on his or her values, the criminal organization may add that if the employee does not accept the bribe, family members may get hurt or worse. The forced acceptance of the bribe leads to a stronger connection between the employee and the outside organization, as independent from the treat, the acceptance of money means a violation of law, including personal consequences, if this relation would be made transparent to authorities.[22]

1.2.4 Protect the Dots!

Philosopher and novelist Ayn Rand recognized in her masterpiece "Atlas Shrugged" that corruption leads to the interference of trade and, eventually, to a doomed society.[23] Several different studies and articles confirm the negative consequences and costs of corruption for a country. But it does not stop there. As business is part of society, corruption also dooms the corporate system. The known cases of the past show that it is impossible to control bribery and limit it to just one area or region. Even if corruption is practiced only in receptive sectors and/or countries, it is not a sustainable business strategy. If one dot of the system gets infected with offering or receiving a bribe, analogue to a living organism, the whole company can be infected with the virus of corruption.

---

[22] Henz, Patrick (2019): "Compliance is a Race Car."

[23] Rand, Ayn (1957): "Atlas Shrugged"

Like a viral contagion, corruption will spread throughout an organization if the infected dot cannot be cured on time. In this case, the dot can be an employee, but also an external partner, which connects to the employee, for example, a sales employee of a provider, or a procurement responsible at the client organization. Besides that, a dot can be a circulating message like "be creative" or "this is a must-win project". If there are no clear lines identifiable, such messages may pressure employees, as they may do not understand what is expected from them by management. A message not only includes the spoken or written word, but also observed behavior. An adequate "tone from the topic" is imperative to ensure a non-toxic corporate atmosphere. Another source of infection could be the corporate tools, regulations and guidelines. If these processes are not addressing the risk of corruption or are over-protective and over -bureaucratic, they may tempt employees to non-adequate behavior. Deming defined this effect with *"A bad system will beat a good person every time."* A clear and simple message must provide the antibiotic called "zero tolerance." To illustrate this point, let us imagine that a sales employee pays a bribe to a procurement person at a potential customer's company to ensure a project win. From this point in the decision-making process, the combination of price and quality plays only a subordinate role. The winning factor is the bribe. Inside the selling company, the impact is a decline in the importance of production and project management relative to sales. Management attention and employee focus shifts to sales, as this function is considered most valuable for the company.

Corruption entering from the sales departments also directly affect the colleagues in production and project management. They are less motivated, as they feel they are no longer valued. In response, these teams produce lower-quality work. Poor motivation leads to a decreased sense of employee loyalty, which can result in higher rates of theft, sabotage, internal fraud and employee turnover. Meanwhile, management loses interest in how tasks are achieved, preferring instead to focus only on sales results. The virus easily spreads from department to department, from dot to dot. The growing infection soon spreads to the procurement department. The holistic view gets lost, as the internal priority is clearly the "successful" sales department. Due to this, procurement loses its independence and is now advised by sales. Procurement is pushed to use certain providers, based on whether the bribery model requires a third party or if the supplier is a family member of the prospective customer. As with the production team, we find the same effects of employee demotivation.

The opposite sides of the corporate system, Sales and Procurement, are the riskiest parts for infection. Nevertheless, the virus can enter via all dots. For example, key-decision makers at the client organization may request to let their children enter as summer interns; classic blue-collar workers may get bribed to sabotage production, or IT-experts to release a virus into the IT-system.

Corruption is not part of a culture, but a learned behavior often used to create a shortcut through complex legal environments. Many companies have an extensive system of guidelines, policies and tools.

The infection starts effecting the quality of work. Unaware of the bribe, the development team wrongly concludes that the company's solutions are competitive, and that investment is unnecessary. In contrast, competitors that work with full transparency foster the development of better solutions. Over time, the company that succeeds because of bribery loses its competitive edge. To compensate for this weakness, it must increase the size of bribe payments – a situation that the potential recipients exploit. Eventually, the bribes are not large enough to justify the difference in competitiveness. And if a significant number of talented employees have left to work at another company, it will be difficult to switch strategies to foster the development of superior products or identify less costly production methods. By this time, the virus has also infected the bribed company. Because of bribe payments, the procurement employee has selected a sub-optimal solution for the company. Now this company is not using the best and/or the most cost-effective materials for its own production. It becomes less competitive and no longer offers attractive solutions. A sales employee working for the bribed company needs to find another factor to win business, and may be tempted to offer a bribe. You can kill the virus. If we see a company as a living organism, then a preventive treatment should be prescribed for this disease. Ethics & Compliance workshops can work much like vaccinations. With relevant case discussions and role-playing exercises, employees can learn about potential situations they could face, how to react, and what consequences could occur.

Bureaucracy provokes corruption and vice versa. To avoid this downward spiral, a company should establish internal processes that are as simple as possible to ensure transparency and employee accountability. Ethics & Compliance Officers cannot do their jobs only from behind closed office doors. They must be easy to reach and well-known across the company. Trusted and highly connected employees can take on the additional role of a "Compliance Ambassador," and IT tools can ensure that an anonymous reporting system is available 24 hours a day. Compliance training sessions cannot be limited to presentations about rules and regulations. It they are, employees will only behave if they feel controlled. Instead, companies need to establish a values-based culture where employees understand their role inside the organization and how corruption could affect their job. In this culture, everyone is equipped to face difficult situations – and not just employees in typical risk groups such as sales or procurement. Is your company protected against this kind of "corruption contagion"? What kinds of "vaccinations" does your company have in place to stave off bribery and corruption?

In business psychology literature, group pressure is often presented as a risk factor, but it can be used also for the benefit of the company. The classic experiment to demonstrate group pressure is the conformity experiment by Solomon Asch. The experiment leader presented three lines to the participants, each with a different length. Then the students saw a second card with just one line. Their task was to tell, which of the first three lines had the same length as the one from the second card. A basic task, as the differences had been obvious. But only the last student was really a participant. The other ones had been involved into the experiment and consciously gave a wrong answer. Interesting in Asch's experiment, in most of the cases, the independent last participant repeated the earlier wrong answers.[24] This behavior could be interpreted in several ways. Sometimes the participant gave consciously the wrong answer, as he or she was afraid to discuss this with the group and defend the own point of view. In other cases, the independent participant observed the earlier answers from the group and started to doubt his or her own perception. Now the participant gave the same answer as the other participants, but with the idea that this was really the correct one.

---

[24] Asch, Solomon (1951): "Effects of group pressure on the modification and distortion of judgments"

This effect can be used to create a positive group pressure. Communication, training and workshops are not only to be used to inform and train employees, but also are an ideal channel to communicate a positive corporate message. If a certain number of employees are reached and convinced, so that they really live a stand up-culture, these employees commit a positive peer pressure to the still not convinced ones. Of course, the tone from the top is most relevant, but the additional group pressure works from all levels, also lower level employees can influence higher ones. This is an argument to limit Compliance workshops and events not only to potential high-risk groups, but extend the invitation to all employees. Inside the corporate system, positive group pressure can be understood as "herd immunity of the dots". Even if a single dot is infected by the corruption virus, the protected dots around it avoid the spreading of the virus.

For a positive and open corporate culture, it is mandatory to limit potential Compliance risks. Not only that we create a "stand-up" culture, but all employees are involved. The atmosphere often (but not always) starts with the tone from the top. Employees from all levels can be a positive example. Colleagues with less strong values and attitudes get influenced by them. This for their operational tasks, and hopefully the perceived positive environment will change the employee's mindset and foster his or her values.[25]

---

[25] Henz, Patrick (2017): "Wirtschaftspsychologie & Compliance"

The Canadian singer and songwriter included two particular lines into his song "Anthem":
"There is crack in everything.
That's how the light gets in."[26]

Rarely he explained the meaning of his music, nevertheless in one of these few occasions he commented that a crack can be in everything, *"physical objects, mental objects, constructions of any kind."*[27] Organizations must be aware that a system never can reach perfection. It is impossible to shield employees against the temptations of the environment, resumed by Donald Cressey with "pressure", "opportunity" and "rationalization".[28] Inside dots use the crack to connect with outside dots. The same is valid for positive values, which can lead to higher employee activity in society to support stronger labor rights, AI ethics or environmental protection. To ensure that the appearance of cracks do not lead to internal conflicts, companies must establish internal spaces, where employees and management can get into open, critical and constructive discussion. This with the goal to use the energy and knowledge for the best interest of the company.

---

[26] Cohen, Leonard (1992): "Anthem"

[27] Werber, Cassie (2016): „"There is a crack in everything, that's how the light gets in": The story of Leonard Cohen's "Anthem""

[28] Cressey, Donald (1973): "Other People's Money: A Study in the Social Psychology of Embezzlement"

The more interaction inside an organization, the easier infected dots can transmit the virus of corruption to their colleagues. Infections can occur based on interaction with outside dots, but also with new employees starting inside the company. Due to this, Ethics & Compliance questions should be a part of recruitment interviews and tests. If companies seek candidates for higher level positions, adequate background checks shall be done.

1.2.5 The Gonk Risk

The Internet of Things is the actual trend to connect all smart devices to the internet, or at least a Cloud. This includes computers, laptops, phones, TVs, but also devices with a "lower smartness", such as wearables, washing machines or printers. A world, where machines with different levels of intelligence co-existed already had been presented by the original 1977 Star Wars movie. Of course, C-3P0 and R2-D2 had been part of the lead characters, but George Lucas created a big diversity of droids, and not all of them spoke fluently over 6 million languages as the golden robot.[29]

Especially the power droids became a fan favorite. They are not a classic droid, more a mobile power generator. Due to this, its Artificial Intelligence was limited, what included its communication skills. The machine was only capable to produce "gonk"-like sounds, what also became the droid's nickname.

---

[29] Lucas, George (1977): "Star Wars"

In today's networks printers are such a gonk-like device. They are connected to the Cloud for our convenience. Automatically they send a message to the manufacturer to ensure that the client receives on time the new ink. For this task the machine does not need a sophisticated AI. This makes these devices vulnerable for hacker-attacks. Relevant, as users may send confidential documents wire-less to the device to print them out.

Furthermore, hackers may emulate the behavior a gonk-device, as a printer, washing machine, refrigerator or toy to get access to a network. If this is established, the faked device may get used to enter a virus into the network. Damage could be a full shut-down of the system or that the refrigerator orders food delivered to a different address. Not only a challenge for the anti-virus software, but also the user, as not all devices should get automatically added to the company- or home-network.

1.2.6 Zero Trust Networks: Employees interlinked

"Zero trust security is an IT security model that requires strict identity verification for every person and device trying to access resources on a private network, regardless of whether they are sitting within or outside of the network perimeter. No single specific technology is associated with zero trust; it is a holistic approach to network security that incorporates several different principles and technologies."[30] The market research company Forrester developed this concept based on the understanding that it is impossible to ensure that single parts of the networks had not been hacked. For this, the best protection is to keep all parts as isolated as possible. This

---

[30] Cloudfare (fetched 23.12.2019)

in opposite to the earlier philosophy "trust but verify."[31]

Vladimir Nabokov's novel from 1962 "Pale Fire" included a 999-line poem by a fictional poet. Four lines prominently appeared more than 50 years later in the science fiction movie "Blade Runner 2049":

"A system of cells interlinked within

Cells interlinked within cells interlinked

Within one stem. And dreadfully distinct

Against the dark, a tall white fountain played."

The book's fictive author shortly interpreted these lines:

"A system, etc.

The fitting-in of the threefold "cells interlinked" is most skillfully managed, and one derives logical satisfaction from the "system" and "stem" interplay."

The movie uses this small part of the poem as a test-procedure for the replicant K to ensure that he did not develop emotions as reaction to his job, the eliminating of other replicants. Such would question his ability to continue with the tasks. Only zero emotions ensured the efficient execution of the job, being a perfect part of the system.

In opposite to these genetically engineered replicants, humans cannot switch off emotions, as they are deep inside us since early steps of evolution. New-born babies begin

---

[31] Forrester (fetched 03.01.2020): "Zero Trust"

their cognitive journey and are helpless without a caregiver. To nevertheless stay comfortable in this situation, their instincts give them a complete trust into their parents. Trough the various stages of socialization, the individuals learn that trust could get misused, but in general, trust inside the different groups turns out as a useful construct.

Companies connect individuals out of numerous local and social groups. Due to this, it is necessary to implement a system of internal processes. Various tools have the task to organize corporate decisions based on authority and knowledge. Emotional preferences should be faded out at this stage. Nevertheless, employees understand how to infuse this into system.

Pernille Rudlin, expert on Japanese business and corporate cultures explains "Shinrai", the Japanese concept for "trust": *"It is composed of two characters, shin, meaning "believe", and rai, which means "to request". In other words, if you trust someone, you believe they will do what you request."*[32] For example, if various approvers are possible, the employees seek not automatically the one with the highest knowledge, but the one most likely to approve, which could be based on a positive mutual relation.

W. Edwards Deming acknowledged that *"a bad system can beat a good employee every time."* If the system is perceived as a bureaucratic burden, employees develop a negative attitude to it. As result, the individuals look for loopholes inside the regulations. Looking to comply with the words of the

---

[32] Rudlin, Pernille (2019): "The five elements of building trust between Japanese and European business cultures"

guideline, but not its spirit or intention. If efficient controls are missing, employees will try to bypass the system. To achieve this position, rules must leave enough space for the heart. This is no contradiction, as guidelines could be designed to include this freedom. Furthermore, clear rules can protect the employees, as they can act based on their values inside the defined safe space.

Even if the system itself is emotional-less, it can be emotionally loaded. Its owner shall give an adequate tone-from-top, ensuring transparency of processes, including explaining the reason for the various sub-systems and approval-requirements. It must be clear that its purpose is to protect company and employees. As smooth usage is in everybody's best interest, user-feedback should be considered to further develop the system. On the other hand, employees must understand that the defined processes are mandatory, and deviations lead to consequences. The network interlinks the users, organizing the efficient execution of tasks. This may include emotion, as employees may identify alternatives inside the processes.

Zero trust networks want to avoid the misuse of trust between different IT-applications with the including of an authorization-process for each connection. As humans are vulnerable, processes insist for each usage to identify themselves (for example via the visible usage of the ID-batch inside the office location), but due to human trust, many times such requirements get violated in mutual agreement, as the regulations not get fostered by management.

Already back in 1999, David Bowie predicted the impact of internet: *"I don't think we've even seen the tip of the iceberg. I think the potential of what the internet is going to do to society, both good and bad is unimaginable… it's an alien life form."*[33] Group interaction, including perceived pressure can lead to accelerated decisions. A risk factor, especially for decisions with a higher risk level. To ensure that employees are aware of their individual responsibility, to take accountability, their connections must include a designed stop, where only an active decision can continue the process. To make this efficient, employees should liberate themselves from the perceived interlinks, including separate themselves from the concept of trust, but purely decide on required information; a "zero trust network."

If we understand Bowie's prediction not only as analyzing the internet, but complex systems in general, we can conclude that a system grows and acts like a living organism (Gaia-theory). Like the blob, non-consciously it seeks the perfect fit to the ecosystem. Due to this, it is important that society (laws) and direct shareholders including

---

[33] BBC Newsweek (2019): "Interview with David Bowie"

management infuse conscious (vision and values) into the system, to ensure sustainability.

Later in the Blade Runner 2049-movie, a scene lets us hear Elvis Presley: *"We can't go on together with suspicious minds,"*[34] a reminder that zero trust is against human psychology. For this, companies should not implement not-necessary authorization processes. Continuous risk-assessments should analyze the week-points of the organization, and regular training of its employees avoid an over-trust into technology, but also other humans. An efficient system can also reduce group-pressure. Decisions cannot be taken inside the flow of a discussion, but must be done via the tools of a system, including a four-eyes-principle or other system-approvals.

There is no one-fits-all answer to the question how much employees should trust each other, or also other dots like external stakeholders, technology or communication. Critical thinking must be kept up to reduce the risk of internal frauds, accidental leaks or also cognitive attacks. Trust is part of being human, therefore controls should not eliminate such, the opposite, trust must build up for the system itself.

---

[34] James, Mark (1968): "Suspicious Minds"

1.2.7 Cressey 4.0

To reach their goal to enter the protected network, hackers are searching for the weakest brick in the wall. Due to this, most modern attacks are not done by autonomous software, but "cognitive hacks". These are semi-automated attacks, mostly known as "phishing emails", where the hackers want the user to convince to visit a link or directly open an attachment. Of course, webpages or attachments are not what they pretend to be, but the user gives his or her bank information to an unauthorized person or directly activates a dangerous virus.

Apart from this illegal practices, computers and persuasion also exist in the grey area called "Captology". The term is based on Stanford University scientist B.J. Fogg, who started to investigate a type of software, what tries to persuade its users to show certain desired actions. Today the university has an own laboratory dedicated to Captoloy.[35]

The technique follows the rules of cognitive learning, as the user receives for each desired behavior an award. But in opposite to the original experiments, such awards are mostly virtual without a direct value, such as likes or virtual contacts. The GPS community "Waze" works like this, as with each reported traffic jam, the user receives points and small awards, which can include different car designs on the map.

---

[35] Stanford University (fetched 30.06.2020): "Stanford Persuasive Tech Lab"

Other Captology strategies include that the user does not have to click actively to start something, but must do something to stop the process. Streaming platforms as "Netflix" feature an autorun-function, what (if not deactivated in the preferences), let the next episode of the series start automatically.[36]

Based on "Gamification"-approach, apps can motivate the user to keep in the process. This with telling him or her how much is still missing to stay on the current level or approach to the next one. Activision included such rewards in their 80s video games for the Atari system. For example, after completing five rounds in "Enduro"[37] or reaching 20,000 points in "Pitfall!",[38] you could take a photo of the screenshots and send it via letter to the local Activision publisher. With this, the company sent you badge, a worthy trophy to present to your friends! "Uber" uses a similar approach. If drivers want to quit for the day, the app automatically advised how much is missing to reach the desired daily salary or even to achieve a higher. Often such messages motivate the user to continue for one or two drives more. Of course, the users benefit from change of behavior, but on the other hand, this can go on the costs of social contacts, as family life. Subconsciously, the user gets "bribed", as the app tries that the human violates the original work-life-balance. Such based on a classic management approach as: *"You can't manage people. You can*

[36] Stoecker, Christian (2017): "Werden Sie Teil der Maschine"

[37] Miller, Larry (1983): "Enduro"

[38] Crane, David (1982): "Pitfall!"

bribe 'em".[39]

As both, Cognitive Hacks and Captology want to manipulate the user to bypass internal guidelines, attitudes or even values, they are understood as temptations. Similar as Donald Cressey already defined in its famous "Fraud Triangle".[40]

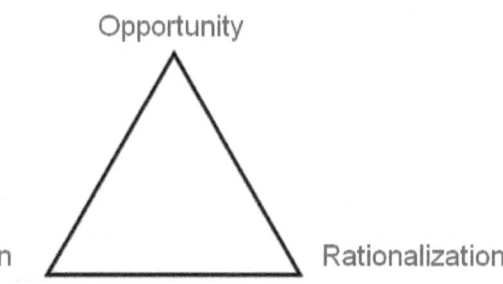

The opportunity is a temptation to "act without thinking". The software pretends to know what is in the user's best interest and offers an easy solution to stay in the personal comfort zone. A critical development, as machines can drag humans into their world, as they try to deactivate or limit the decision-making process and let them act like trained robots.

Such "automated employees" are a risk factor of the company, as they lost temporary their ability to question themselves and others. Violation of internal guidelines or

---

[39] Iverson, Kenneth (1998)

[40] Crassey, Donald (1973): "Other People's Money: A Study in the Social Psychology of Embezzlement"

external laws are relevant risk factor for the organization.

Based on this, data privacy and cyberattacks, are not a pure IT topic, but Compliance is responsible to protect the company and employees. US president Abraham Lincoln once said in his annual message to the Congress from December 1862 that *"we must rise with the occasion."*[41] Spam-filters and anti-virus software cannot protect the employees against phishing emails or non-IT-based "social engineering". Therefor training and workshops are required to foster the individual's knowledge and motivate him or her to not blindly trust an email or software, but, if possible, take the conversation from the virtual to the real world, as strange information from the email should be verified at least with a telephone-call. Even if it is not a classic topic, based on his or her reputation and experience, the Ethics & Compliance Officer can take the responsibility for the organization & employees.

1.3 Knowledge about variation

1.3.1 Smart Contracts

W. Edwards Deming started as an electrical engineer, so no surprise that he kept the ideas of connections and electric circuits also as he became a business consultant. One of his well-known theories is the "System of Profound Knowledge". A concept that defines that an organization is nothing else than a holistic system, not only connecting

---

[41] Lincoln, Abraham (1862): "Annual Message to the Congress"

internal resources, but also interlinking with external stakeholders. For managing the system, four pillars are relevant: Appreciation of a system, knowledge of variation, theory of knowledge, psychology.[42]

Deming published this concept back in 1993. Nevertheless, the philosophy sounds more modern than ever before. Thanks to Digital Twins, his philosophy can now be practically implemented; not only in production facilities, but also office environment. Generation Z (born 1997 and later)[43] is in the process to enter the actual work-force. These employees not only grew up with the internet, but also had been socialized with voice assistants and other Artificial Intelligence. Accordingly, they appreciate the technology, as they know interacting with AI (understandable as a mathematical system) to receive the required results. With Generation Z, the future work-force is skilled in system-thinking, which applies also for the Legal & Compliance-department.

The concept of smart contracts was first defined one year after the "System of Profound Knowledge", not by a lawyer, but the computer scientist Nick Szabo: *"A smart contract is a computerized transaction protocol that executes the terms of a contract. The general objectives of smart contract design are to satisfy common contractual conditions (such as payment terms, liens, confidentiality, and even enforcement), minimize exceptions both malicious and*

---

[42] Deming, W. Edwards (1993): "The New Economics for Industry, Government, Education"

[43] Dimock, Michael (2019): "Defining generations: Where Millennials end and Generation Z begins"

accidental, and minimize the need for trusted intermediaries. Related economic goals include lowering fraud loss, arbitration and enforcement costs, and other transaction costs.[44] As mathematician, his definition of a legally binding document is nothing else than a rules-based algorithm.

With extraterritorial laws such as the US Foreign Corrupt Practices Act[45] or the UK Modern Slavery Act 2015,[46] companies can hold responsible for their vendors, sales agents and other partners. As consequence, they shall elaborate a code of conduct for vendors, in parallel conduct background checks and request evidence. The electronic signature on a contract is based on conditions. If a vendor stops complying with one or more of them, like the effect that an electric circuit gets interrupted, also the validness of the contract is not given anymore. For example, a company may request from its vendors to upload an annual statement that their products are free of conflict minerals. Based on this condition, the agreement was signed. If the vendor not complies with the deadline of the rule, the smart contract gets automatically abrogated until the topic gets solved or the company decides to terminate the agreement.

Smart contracts can be combined with continuous monitoring, where an algorithm connects automatically with various data-bases to check if a used vendor gets listed or delisted from a governmental sanction-list, is involved

---

[44] Szabo, Nick (1994): "Smart Contracts"

[45] The United States Department of Justice (1977): "Foreign Corrupt Practices Act"

[46] UK Legislation (2015): "Modern Slavery Act 2015"

into a law-case, or negatively mentioned in the news what could lead to reputational risk.

The ideal collaboration of AI with humans is that the machine is responsible for the level 1-tasks, so that the human expert can focus on the level 2-priorities. Regarding smart contracts, this means that the algorithm can continuously monitor that all defined rules are still valid. The moment the AI perceives that this is not the case anymore, it interrupts the smart-contract and alerts the employee to analyze the situation. The human stays in charge, and accordingly must make final decisions to confirm or disconfirm the computer-alert. This requires not only that the human understands the system, but also that he/she is able of critical thinking to avoid falling to the automation bias or a general over-trust into the AI. Deming's focus on human psychology inside the system is imperative.

A contract is *"a voluntary, deliberate, and legally binding agreement between two or more competent parties. Contracts are usually written but may be spoken or implied, and generally have to do with employment, sale or lease, or tenancy."*[47] This broad definition applies also for smart contracts. The province of Alberta nevertheless published the "Electronic Transactions Act",[48] proclaimed in force in 2003. The law defines the validness of electronic contracts, including the option of *"the interaction of an electronic agent and a person or by the interaction of electronic agents."* Today the wording "electronic agent" is not

---

[47] BusinessDictionary (fetched 04.04.2020): "contract"

[48] Open Government (2019): "Electronic Transactions Act"

common anymore, but can be translated as automated or even autonomous software.

As the wills of all included parties must be ensured, auditability of such a dynamic contract (which could be temporary non-valid) for all points of time must be given. Modern definitions align smart contracts with blockchain: *"A smart contract is a self-executing contract with the terms of the agreement between buyer and seller being directly written into lines of code. The code and the agreements contained therein exist across a distributed, decentralized blockchain network. The code controls the execution, and transactions are trackable and irreversible."*[49]

The blockchain technology promises enhanced cyber-protection for smart contracts, as the information does not get stored on just one server, but is encrypted and decentralized on numerous ones. The different machines validate each other, and any deviating information (as a manipulated contract), would be automatically overwritten with the correct authorized information stored on the other servers. As expressed by "chain", no information gets deleted, but all changes registered with the day and time. If the smart contract could connect automatically with other databases, where certifications are stored as blockchain, the contract would add those. If not, it could connect to an internal server, where vendors manually upload such documents.

In times of global anti-corruption enforcement and rising stakeholder activism, companies want to ensure that their partners continuously comply with the law and defined

---

[49] Frankenfield, Jake (2019): "What is a Smart Contract?"

human rights-initiatives. As result, more documentation and statements are required. Smart contracts are a possibility to achieve transparency, and automatically control the needed certifications. In the spirit of W. Edwards Deming, they are a bridge to connect two organizational systems.

As discussed earlier, an organization cannot be sharply divided from its ecosystem. Thinking into the other direction, different departments or sub-parts could be managed like independent cost-centers. If so, blockchain and smart contracts could be also used to connect internal sub-systems.

1.3.2 Change

Conformity pressure had been confirmed by different classic experiments, as for example by the Conformity[50] or the Stanford Prison experiment.[51] Different social levels perceive different types of pressure.

- Leaders feel less pressure than lower levels inside the group. Often it is quite the opposite; they see the position as self-realization (aligned with Maslow's Hierarchy of Needs[52]) and like to show individualism.

---

[50] Asch, Salomon E.: (1951): "Effects of group pressure on the modification and distortion of judgments."

[51] Zimbardo, Philip G. (1971): "The power and pathology of imprisonment"

[52] Maslow, Abraham (1943): "A Theory of Human Motivation"

- Another group, who feels less conformity pressure, are the outsiders, which are no direct part of the main group.

Conformity pressure normally works that the individual adapts to the behavior of the main group, but the effect can also get reversed. Then the individual or the small group can influence the big group and can trigger a change of behavior, including attitudes or values. This applies for the situation that the individual or the small group is higher involved in the topic than the main group. Thanks to its small size, knowledge and involvement, they can work more efficient than the big group. With this they can convince increasingly of the other group's members, at least if they have logical arguments.

Dots (employees) get influenced by the number of dots around them, by the perceived distance (another employee to be perceived by near and like yourself), by their status (someone one a higher level to be admired, but not feared) and the energy of other employee.

In times of Covid-19 so-called "super-spreaders" infected a higher number of people due to their extensive number of connections. A similar effect could be used for change management. To switch from "push" to "pull", company management can implement change-agents to the different parts of the organization. These should be highly motivated ("energized") employees, which are able to motivate their peers for the coming change. This with informing, including help to understand why the planned change is necessary, as it is in the best interest for the organization, but also each single employee.

These findings we can apply for a company's internal change management, as to be successful it requires to have

- top management as sponsor,
- a convincing and strong concept,
- the tasks be driven by a small effective group and
- this group acts independent from other departments to avoid perceived conflicts of interest.

1.4 Theory of Knowledge

1.4.1 Curiosity for Machine Learning

One part of behavioral science aims to explain how people learn to execute certain scripts to execute in different situations. In the theory of conditioning, after a defined behavior, individuals receive a reinforcement. As people want to receive this reward on a continuous base, they try to repeat the earlier behavior. For example, parents reward their children for positive results at school, or later companies reward employees with salary, if they complied with the requirements of their job-profile.

As individuals perceive the need to have a positive self-image, often they start to appreciate the actions, even if there are no reinforcements anymore. For example, students get curious and like learning itself, even if parents would not continue reinforcement of positive grades.

Reinforcement learning is not only used for animals and humans, but also machine learning. Artificial Intelligence is not able to perceive a cognitive relation between action and reward, so classically depends on the identifying of a statistical relation. The more direct the relation between action and reinforcement, the easier it is for the algorithm to identify such. This enables AI to master classic video games, such as Ms. Pac Man, and there beat all human players. In opposite to this, AI has problems with games like Montezuma's Revenge, as the game-play does not includes regular rewards for the player. As mixture between puzzle and jump-and-run, players are stuck in a Mexican pyramid, and have to collect keys and other items, together with unlocking doors. In the beginning AI failed, as it could not detect statistical relations between its own try-and-error behavior and the non-regular reinforcement. So far, human players had been superior, as they not depend on conditioning, but can solve the puzzles based on cognitive understanding.

Researcher by OpenAI used a trick. They programmed curiosity inside the AI. This included a "self-rewarding" inside the algorithm, so the AI perceived a reward not only for collecting items (external), but also for exploring (internal) as much as possible of the pyramids. Programmed internal motivation made the AI less depended from external reinforcement. The artificial curiosity lead to positive results, as thanks to the combination of the new behavior together with exact execution of movements, the AI became superior in comparison to human competitors.

1.4.2 Continuous Learning

When Deming spoke about the "theory of knowledge" he meant C.I. Lewis' definition of "Pragmatism", which he later re-labeled to "Epistemology" (Greek for: knowledge logical discourse). Related to big philosophers like Buddha, Confucius, Kant, Nietze or Plato, Epistemology studies the nature of knowledge, justification and the rationality of belief. One of Deming's famous quotes is: *"Without data, you're just another person with an opinion."* Later he underlined the importance of the theory in a letter to fellow statistician Ronald D. Moen, where he classified the known "Plan-Do-Check-Act"-circle (PDCA, comparable to a statistical relation between input and output) as "corruption".[53] In opposite to this he developed, or at least contributed to, the "Plan-Do-Study-Act"-system (PDSA, comparable to a

---

[53] Deming W. Edwards (1990): "Personal letter to Ronald D. Moen"

logical relation).[54][55] Checking compares results with requirements. Studying goes one step further, as the results trigger learning, leading to new knowledge, which updates not only the process, but also the requirements. Since the very beginning, even before taking the first steps, humans are curious. A circumstance, which parents and teachers must foster, and not discourage. Not only relevant for the educational system, but also companies. Finishing education and entering the first job, young employees are motivated "to change the world". A feeling which easily could be destroyed due to bureaucratic over-burden or a corporate culture, which seeks to keep the status quo, discouraging challenging it. Especially in times of uncertainty, where it is predicted that students will work tomorrow in jobs not existing today, it is imperative that humans keep up their natural born-curiosity. As companies depend on this human characteristic, they must support their employees. This could have different forms, like paying (partly) for courses, or allowing them to use work-time for training or self-selected projects ("learning by doing"). Technology can be used, like "opportunity marketplaces",[56] to change corporate training from "push" to "pull".

---

[54] Moen, Ronald D. / Norman, Clifford L. (2010): "circling back"

[55] Henz, Patrick (2019): "Tomorrow's Business Ethics: Philip K. Dick vs. W. Edwards Deming"

[56] Schrage, Michael / Schwartz, Jeff / Kiron, David / Jones, Robin / Buckley, Natasha (2020): "Opportunity Marketplaces"

1.4.3 Curiosity leads to Empathy

Curiosity is not only imperative to ensure continuous learning, keeping employees qualified for the job. It also is required to keep the individuals acting on their personal values. Perceptions and prejudices like "corruption is a faceless crime" or "corruption is a part of culture" are based on missing information, and lacking understanding of interconnections. It is not, that relevant articles are not out there, even for free at the internet, but often individuals are satisfied with their current status of knowledge and not want to invest into further information seeking. Such behavior could be observed in regions, where corruption could be observed in the media, but it does not have a relevant impact on the individuals' lives. Due to the missing predicted impact on the result of further information about corruption, such individuals are not motivated, for example, to start an extended decision-making process for projects in higher risk regions. This not only leads to ethical concerns, but also legal risks, as independent where companies conduct business, they are liable to their home anti-corruption laws, and in addition also to the US FCPA[57] and the UK Bribery Act.[58] The last at least, if they have the slightest connection to these two countries. To reduce the risk of non-adequate behavior when employees are abroad or involved into business on the other side of the world, the Ethics & Compliance Officer has not only to inform about rules and regulations. As complete control is not possible,

---

[57] The United States Department of Justice (1977): "Foreign Corrupt Practices Act"

[58] UK Legislation (2015): "Modern Slavery Act 2015":

employees must understand why such regulations had been created, and what are the negative effects of corruption on societies. For example, as defined by Paolo Mauro: *"Corruption may distort the composition of government expenditure. Corruption may tempt government officials to choose government expenditures less on the basis of public welfare than the opportunity they provide for extorting bribes."*[59]

Children are born curious, so a logical way to teach adults to become curious again is via gamification of corporate training or workshops. In a fun way, employees can simulate different scenarios testing potential behavior (Deming's variation) to study the outcomes. That way they learn to appreciate the company's Compliance system, as they understand how it protects the company and them, but in parallel also the markets and societies. Due to Alexandre C. Serpa, pioneer in creating Compliance board games up to retro videos games, *"the most important aspect of the game is not winning it, it is all about challenging preconceptions, asking 'why' questions."*[60]

[59] Mauro, Paulo (1997)" Why worry about Corruption?"

[60] Serpa, Alexandre C. (2020): "Compliance Board Games"

"Veritas Vincat – Operation Compliance", photo with friendly permission of Alexandre C. Serpa.

One of Artificial Intelligence's advantages is its superior ability to analyze data, detect patterns, and use this information for prediction. Depending from case to case, the algorithm may get highly accurate, nevertheless biased data may lead to flawed forecasts. Especially when predictions are about humans and human behavior, error rates mean ethical dilemmas. In opposite to AI, humans are uncapable to evaluate a high number of data, especially if coming in continuous streams from a high number of sensors. Due to this, humans predict less based on statistical relations, but based on information and knowledge with the aim to understand the logical relations. As humans and algorithms work differently, we need to align them inside a Human AI-Team, while the human stays in charge.

Humans can automate some of their tasks to algorithms, including Robotic Process Automaton (RPA). The employee defines the rules, and the algorithms can act and decide accordingly. The AI accelerates decision-making. As conclusion, it requires adequate oversight by the human co-worker.

1.5 Psychology

1.5.1 Coffee Beans

Perceived time-pressure tempts employees to keep the seek of information short and captured inside the box, avoiding the processing of needed new data. In addition, tasks perceived as routine may lead to an underestimation of risks and overtrust into standard solutions and recommendations of an Artificial Intelligence. To avoid, or at least reduce, these behavioral biases, experts suggest having a break before taking a decision.

If possible, sleep a night before making a relevant decision. Even if potential consequences are less important, the "cup of coffee"-rule should be obeyed. A small disruption of the routine can be used to speak with a friend, family-member or colleague; this often with a cup of coffee or tea. Depending on the confidentiality level of the decision, it can be discussed with a second person to get a different opinion based on diverse knowledge and experience.

Covid-19 disrupts actual the business and keeps employees working from home. So far, it is unknown how the "new normal" will look like, but it is questionable if big open offices will ever return. It is less that this disruption leads to a different reality, but it acts as an accelerator for the already existing trend towards more home-office. On the other hand, this also takes away the possibility of short non-formal talks, this to get a different opinion or the latest "office news".

Two startups understand the need and offer virtual solutions. The first is a social network from Italy: #pausacaffè. Its claim is to offer a break for smart-workers. It not only offers useful information about "agile work" and work-life balance, but also organizes short online meetings, where interested members, of course with a cup of coffee, can connect (via Zoom and Google Hangouts) and discuss a topic. Most of employees have at home a better coffee-machine (including higher quality beans) than at the office, what strengthens the experience. In opposite to classic social media platforms, pausacaffè motivates the people to have a talk with relative strangers (just seeing the short profile). This like the office, where employees speak with their friends and direct contacts, but also other colleagues.

The second platform comes from California. Online Town is a video-calling space that lets multiple people hold separate conversations in parallel. The platform simulates a complete office setup, with its office-desks and different types of meeting rooms. The 2D-graphic not only connects to actual retro design, as homage to the late 1980s and '90s, but furthermore has the advantage that users can run the application directly inside the browser, without special requirements for hardware or connection. Similar as in the physical world, Online Town works by fading each user's audio and video based on how far they are from each other. With this, it focuses on non-formal meetings, also as options as presenting PowerPoint-slides or screens is missing. Like #pausacaffè, also this digital platform aims to have an anchor in the physical world. The developers are working on a bracelet as wearable, which can indicate if friends or colleagues are online and available for a chat. Coffee is not only needed to ensure reflection inside the system, but to create it itself.

"Think of us as espresso beans. We are also from around the world, but because it is the process more than the ingredients that creates an iconic product of Italian culture and lifestyle.", said by Klaus Busse.

At the 2020 world premiere of the Alfa Romeo Tonale Concept, the company's first hybrid plugin-model, the Head of Design for Fiat, Abarth, Lancia, Alfa Romeo, Maserati at FCA Fiat Chrysler Automobiles Klaus Busse explained his understanding of an efficient system.

What can be more Italian than enjoying a good espresso? Busse compared the international team of talented designers to espresso beans. To create an iconic product of Italian culture and lifestyle, the process is more important than the ingredients.

With this he aligns with W. Edwards Deming concept of the "System of Profound Knowledge" and also Chess Grand Master Garry Kasparov, who concluded: "Weak human + machine + better process was superior to a strong computer alone and, more remarkably, superior to a strong human + machine + inferior process." As consequence, human employees get not directly replaced by algorithms, but employees with superior algorithms replace employees with inferior or none.

The same results could be observed in the Football World Championships, where mostly not the teams with the most famous stars won the title, but the teams without big stars, but diverse players forming a homogeneous team. According to Deming and Kasparov, we can conclude that a superior system is the perfect combination of a team.

Busse added in the presentation that the Alfa Romeo design department "Centro Stilo Alfa Romeo" uses technology to support and accelerate the process, but not lets computers alone design the cars. This as the human designers, due to their experience, are superior in being emphatic with the potential clients.

To create such an efficient system, organizations must investigate their own past to understand core values and comparative advantages. The efficient system must combine employees with each other, but also with equipment, algorithms and business philosophy. Diversity evolves the quality of decisions-making, and the process ensures that the employees all walk into the same direction. This way, internal regulations not limit employees, but protect their creativity, as they define the space where they can live their passion for the job and company.

The process supports the human to ensure that the company's product is human-centered. As Busse explained, "Alfa Romeo puts the driver at the center."

1.5.2 The Mechanism

In 2018, Netflix streamed its first Brazilian series called "The Mechanism". The platform described it as "loosely inspired by true events", but it was nothing less as the needed artistic dealing with the country's biggest corruption case so far, which plunged its whole economy and political system into a deep crisis.

Being aware of the importance of the series, Netflix started an aggressive marketing campaign, up to installing a fictive corruption shop at the capital Brasilia's airport. In fact, travelers had not been able to buy anything, but in the displays they could see potential products like the book "1001 things to do before you begin house arrest" or "Corrupterminos", the lexicon of corruption.

The Cambridge Dictionary defines "mechanism" with "a way of doing something that is planned or part of a system". W. Edwards Deming defined the "System of Profound Knowledge" including its four key-pillars: 1 - Appreciation for a system, 2 - Knowledge about variation, 3 - Theory of knowledge, and 4 - Psychology. Famously, Deming further once said that "a bad system will beat a good person every time." Due to this, it is important that a corporate system not only connects different functions, but also efficiently employees with other employees, and employees with corporate values and knowledge. The last must include that corruption is no face-less crime, but negatively affects the markets and all society. With this in place, knowledge supports the development of empathy.

The definition "mechanism" gets also used in behavioral science. Triggered by a known stimulus, the individual automatically starts a behavioral script, mostly without questioning if these actions are adequate or not. As scenarios are complex and individuals not want to destroy their positive self-perception, they avoid seeking for additional information, as this may contradict the perceived direct relations without collateral damages. Based on their narrow view, the company and themselves would benefit from the illegal actions and there are no victims, as all other indicators had been ignored and turned off.

Mechanical behavior plunges organizations into the abyss. It is imperative to keep up critical thinking. Inside companies, the Ethics & Compliance Officer can support such with different tailor-made workshops. The information that fraud and corruption sabotage the company's sustainability and affect the total market lead to understanding and even empathy. Especially, if via storytelling employees connect the dots how such behavior affects themselves and their loved ones.

Max Kaiser, President of the Anticorruption Commission of the COPARMEX (Confederation of Employers of the Mexican Republic), published a free online class explaining the system as "The Corruption Mechanism: Elections, Appointments, Public Procurement Systems and Contract Execution". Deming understood that companies need to connect to the outside world to incorporate new knowledge. This regarding, Kaiser's short 17 minutes class is an important resource for all Ethics & Compliance Officers to use for their employee training. Internal workshops must present the risks and explain how the company's ethical processes support the employees. Ethical behavior must be established as default. It must be semi-automatic, but not mechanic. As corruption changes its faces, it is imperative to keep up critical thinking, including practice continuous learning. Thanks to such approaches, interactive ethics & compliance workshops work on a logical and emotional level.

1.5.3 Understanding

The Renaissance universal genius Leonardo da Vinci defined the *"Principles for the Development of a Complete Mind: Study the science of art. Study the art of science. Develop your senses-especially learn how to see. Realize that everything connects to everything else."* Mathematics and art align, for example in the concept of the "golden ratio". The relation between the smaller side "a" and longer side "b" should follow the formula:

$$a/b = (a+b)/a$$

If an artist (independent if painter or photographer) complies with this image division, the viewer perceives the art as harmonious. This theory was first defined by the Greek mathematician Euclid of Alexandria (ca. 360 -280 BC). Renaissance artists and scientist rediscovered antique knowledge and and use it as base to enhance actual wisdom.

Da Vinci used this technique for example for this famous "The Last Supper".

Like time of Renaissance meant a rediscovering of human knowledge, today STEM (science, technology, engineering and mathematics) education is the new buzzword to discuss raising competitiveness in science and technology. The idea is to present these topics more vividly at school to motivate more pupils to choose related topics later at university. The Talking Heads became famous for progressive pop music, which they combined with artistic videos. For this, it is no surprise that their former front-man David Byrne argued that "in order to really succeed in whatever... math and the sciences and engineering and things like that, you have to be able to think outside the box, and do creative problem solving... the creative thinking is in the arts." Arts has been included into the concept (now STEAM) and the schools' timetables. With a further step, educators underline the importance of reading. This as books not only transport information, but furthermore inspire the readers. STREAM explains why business leaders should not only read regarding books and articles, but furthermore science fiction. Many of today's developments had been described a long time before, and tomorrow's risks and opportunities also already had been addressed.

In his last interview, W. Edwards Deming explained in 1993: *"A system cannot understand itself. Understanding comes from outside."* [61] With this, he underlines the importance that the corporate system is adequately connected with the eco-system, as without importing outside knowledge, it cannot develop such understanding, or even wisdom, itself.

Steampunk mean retro-science fiction, where today's authors let their stories play in the time for Industrial Revolution (Industry 1.0). This to create an atmosphere similar to Jules Verne (1828 – 1905), the famous science fiction author that time, which used his art to predict submarines or the Apollo moon-program.

---

[61] Stevens, Tim (1994): "Dr. Deming: 'Management Today Does Not Know What Its Job Is' (Part 2)"

The Designer Alliance between Lucasfilm and Porsche is a wonderful example for the STREAM-philosophy, as designers from both companies accepted the joined task to create a Porsche-based starship to include it into the Star Wars-universe. The combination of science, technology, engineering and mathematics with reading and arts. Industry 4.0 not only enables the fusion, but requests it in order of staying competitive.

Ferrari design director Flavio Manzoni mentioned on different occasions that he likes science fiction, including comic books, 1950's designs of gliding cars, but also art-house movies as "2001: A Space Odyssey"[62] As a private sideline project he designed a futuristic flying car, inspired by typical UFO creations. Flavio convinced the company's 3D modeler Guillermo Vasseur, who elaborated a 3D model out of his sketches. Even if it started as a hobby, this

---

[62] Kubrik, Stanley (1968): "2001: A Space Odyssey"

UFOs directly influenced Flavio's work at Ferrari. As he explained at London's Design Museum to celebrate the special exposition "Ferrari: Under the Skin",[63] the silhouettes of his creations, such as the LaFerrari, the J50 and 488, are shaped based on his UFO-idea, especially the middle-parts.

Mazoni's creations are based on his background as an industrial designer, but inspired by books and art. Back to one of his inspirations, "2001: A Space Odyssey". Does the SpaceX Dragon 2 not remind to the minimalist designs of the movie? The same is valid for the company's spacesuit, which are far more elegant than earlier NASA models. The reason links to the Mexican costume designer José Fernandez, who had been responsible for various well-known movies, such as Alien III, Avengers, Bat Man, Black Panther, Ironman, Planet of the Apes and X-Men.[64]

---

[63] The DESIGN MUSEUM (2019): "Ferrari: Under the Skin"

[64] Ironhead Studios (2020): "Concept Art"

SpaceX Dragon 2, SpaceX press-photo.

Besides his work for major Hollywood productions, furthermore, he collaborated with the outside industries, as he created Draft Punk's signature helmets. Again, it was a helmet what connected him to SpaceX. Fernandez participated 2016 in a competition for helmet-designs for this company, unaware that this was for real space exploration instead of a movie. Elon Musk appreciated the design and commissioned Fernandez' company Ironhead to create a complete spacesuit. Coming from futuristic fictional designs, the new approach offering an elegant, comfortable and practical design breaks with the century old development going back to deep-sea diving. Thanks to creative disruption, the solution provides a broader field of vision, and requires less energy for general movements. The helmets themselves had been nearly completely 3D printed, and include built-in air cooling and a retractable visor. The slim spacesuit features connections for air, water and power.[65]

SpaceX Dragon 2, SpaceX press-photo.

The new creativity also reached SpaceX' partner NASA, which reactivated the 1975 simplistic red NASA-logo, known as the worm design. This exclusively for the first joined mission using the space agency's Falcon 9 and the Dragon 2. Nevertheless, further usage is not out of question.[66]

---

[65] Smith, Lacey (2018): "This tricked-out SpaceX helmet is nearly all 3D printed"

[66] NASA (2020): "The Worm is Back!"

1.5.4 Faked Dots

Science fiction author Philip K. Dick wrote less to predict future technology, but more to discuss the meaning of humanity and reality. One of his most famous works, the novel "Do Androids dream of Electric Sheep?",[67] presented a potential reality, ·where parts of the society had been dehumanized, but showed more human behavior than the majority. Ironically, the manufacturers of these replicants used the claim "more human than human", as presented in the later movie "Blade Runner".[68] The 1985 book "I Hope I Shall Arrive Soon" included ten of Dick's short-stories for a first time in book-form. In addition, a still unpublished essay, where the author wrote: *"Fake realities will create fake humans. Or, fake humans will generate fake realities and then sell them to other humans, turning them, eventually, into forgeries of themselves."*[69]

In 2020, Kathleen M. Carley and her team at Carnegie Mellon University's Center for Informed Democracy & Social Cybersecurity analyzed Twitter and *"identified more than 100 types of inaccurate covid-19 stories and found that not only were bots gaining traction and accumulating followers, but they accounted for 82% of the top 50 and 62% of the top 1,000 influential retweeters."*[70] This calculation included that the rate that these bots had

---

[67] Dick, Philip K. (1968): "Do Androids dream of Electric Sheep?"

[68] Scott, Ridley (1982): "Blade Runner"

[69] Dick, Philip K. (1985): "I Hope I Shall Arrive Soon"

[70] Hao, Karen (2020): "Nearly half of Twitter accounts pushing to reopen America may be bots"

been retweeted by human Twitter users. Human decision making depends on data, information, knowledge and wisdom. This also includes data directly perceived by his / her five senses. The complexity of the internet and social media in general, makes it hard up to impossible to distinguish human from AI accounts. Especially the latter are easy to multiply, which enables the bots to outperform humans. A wrong perception of the majority opinion may lead to group pressures as described by th famous Asch Conformity Experiment.[71]

Deming defined that the corporate system connects to the eco-system. To efficiently do so, employees including their leaders, must be able to identify reality. If not, the system does not connect to the adequate dots, but fictive ones. As consequence, business decisions may be made based on faked information. Data, big and smart, are a relevant good for today's companies. Sources must be vetted, streams protected, and algorithms audited. Furthermore, it must be ensured that humans keep up their ability of critical thinking. This also to reduce the risk of cyber-attacks. Professional hackers are highly efficient organizations, not only knowledgably of IT, but also languages, law and human psychology. Due to this, most attacks are cognitive. For example, via phishing emails and intercepted email-communication, hackers try to manipulate one single employee of the corporate system with the goal that he / she deviates corporate guidelines and processes to change a bank account for a transfer, or opens a door to enter the IT-

---

[71] Asch, Salomon E.: (1951): "Effects of group pressure on the modification and distortion of judgments."

system. The manipulation of the employee works like the classic attack of the wooden horse.[72] The employee perceives a faked reality, and acts on that instead of the objective reality. Such wrong perception may last from few minutes to years, but when realized, often the damage was already done.

One part of behavioral science aims to explain how people learn to execute certain scripts to execute in different situations. In the theory of conditioning, after a defined behavior, individuals receive a reinforcement. As people want to receive this reward on a continuous base, they try to repeat the earlier behavior. For example, parents reward their children for positive results at school, or later companies reward employees with salary, if they complied with the requirements of their job-profile.

As individuals perceive the need to have a positive self-image, often they start to appreciate the actions, even if there are no reinforcements anymore. For example, students get curious and like learning itself, even if parents would not continue reinforcement of positive grades.

Reinforcement learning is not only used for animals and humans, but also machine learning. Artificial Intelligence is not able to perceive a cognitive relation between action and reward, so classically depends on the identifying of a statistical relation. The more direct the relation between action and reinforcement, the easier it is for the algorithm to identify such. This enables AI to master classic video

---

[72] Homer (8th century BC): "Odyssey"

games, such as Ms. Pac Man, and there beat all human players. In opposite to this, AI has problems with games like Montezuma's Revenge, as the game-play does not includes regular rewards for the player. As mixture between puzzle and jump-and-run, players are stuck in a Mexican pyramid, and have to collect keys and other items, together with unlocking doors. In the beginning the AI failed, as it could not detect statistical relations between its own try-and-error behavior and the non-regular reinforcement. So far, human players had been superior, as they not depend on conditioning, but can solve the puzzles based on cognitive understanding.

Researcher by OpenAI used a trick. They programmed curiosity inside the AI. This included a "self-rewarding" inside the algorithm, so the AI perceived a reward not only for collecting items (external), but also for exploring (internal) as much as possible of the pyramids. Programmed internal motivation made the AI less depended from external reinforcement. The artificial curiosity lead to positive results, as thanks to the combination of the new behavior together with exact execution of movements, the AI became superior in comparison to human competitors. The corporate system seeks to optimize itself. This requires that it gets out of relative optimums. Key are the interfaces to humans, as due to their ability of creativity, ingenuity and critical thinking can infuse the system with new knowledge, but also questions.

Erik Brynjofsson, director of the Massachusetts Institute of Technology (MIT) Initiative for Digital Economy, stated: *"AI won't be able to replace most jobs anytime soon. But in almost every industry, people using AI are starting to replace people who don't use AI, and that trend will only accelerate."* Paul Ryan, IBM Watson's UK director of Artificial Intelligence, goes one step further with his prediction that in a few years *"every major decision, business and personal, will be made with the assistance of cognitive technologies."*

To make recommendations as efficient as possible, the virtual assistant must get to know the employee. Comparable to Digital Twins in the manufacturing industry, it needs a virtual manifestation of the person to understand his / her skills, knowledge and opportunities. This leads to the concept of the "Personal Digital Twin"-concept (PDT). The authors Roberto Saracco, Juuso Autiosalo, Derrick de Kerckhove, Francesco Flammini and Louis Nisiotis define that a *"PDT is a representation of various aspects of a person"*. This might include its movements and interactions, but also its health status.[73] For the corporate usage, we can include other relevant information, such as education, character, etc.

The PDT is not a pure philosophical concept, but companies like IBM[74] and SAP[75] investigate about its practical use. Defined by Roberto Saracco, co-chair of the

---

[73] Saracco, Roberto / Autiosalo, Juuso, de Kerckhove, Derrick / Flammini, Francesco / Nisiotis, Louis (2020: "The Role of the Personal Digital Twins in Control of Epidemics"

[74] Matthews, Sky (2018): "Designing better machines: the evolution of a cognitive Digital Twin explained"

[75] Steer, Markus (2018): "Will There Be A Digital Twin For Everything And Everyone?"

IEEE Digital Reality Initiative, such an algorithm goes beyond the mirroring of the physical employee, but would include an artificial intelligence to enable it to act autonomously in the virtual space, acquiring required information or execute routine tasks, like organizing meetings or answer frequently asked questions. With this, the employee can delegate tasks to the PDT, to answer questions in after-hours or on holidays. Such a concept would require active cooperation between employee and PDT, as both have regularly to synchronize, an opportunity where the PDT can teach the employee.[76]

A PDT may understand where the employee is inside the career, where he / she wants to go as next step, and due to this, what is needed to close the gap. Platforms like coursera offer a high number of massive open online courses (MOOCs). The PDT can search the databases of such MOOCs to identify the ones of benefit for the employee, considering potential costs. Depending on the employee's calendar, the PDT will recommend the course, including when to do so. In the past, people got access to others' minds by reading books or attend lectures. Today's MOOCs present the teacher in videos, a narrow form of a digital twin. In future, the PDT of a teacher may be linked to an avatar, so that individuals could meet with a teacher in a virtual reality. Just as Data, the crew-member of the USS Enterprise 1701D, could meet with the virtual Stephen Hawking on the holodeck to discuss scientific and other

[76] Saracco, Roberto (2019): "Applying Cognitive Digital Twins to Professional Education"

questions.[77]

Companies can support this development with the implementation of an internal opportunity marketplace. Such a platform can offer internal training opportunities, but also link to external courses, like MOOCs. Furthermore, it can link to potential internal mentors, presentations, internships etc. The individual employee is an expert about itself. With the possibility of self-selection, companies keep talents motivated and offer them a possibility to grow, as they can choose also training outside their actual responsibilities. If the PDT observes past preferences, behavior, and can connect this with the employee's skills and knowledge, similar to Netflix and Spotify, it can recommend learning possibilities. Nevertheless, the decision stays with the employee. Due to this, corporate training shifts from a mandatory compliance with the given, to an empowered employee, who is investing into itself.[78] If we take the STREAM approach, science, technology, engineering and mathematics should connect with reading and arts. Consequently, an opportunity marketplace may include also links to the local theater and museums. It can recommend books and movies. Like the many public open mini-libraries all over the planet, companies may set up a shelf with books and movies. Up to the possibility that employees may donate here their read books. On the other hand, companies may control such donations, as they may

---

[77] Singer, Alexander (1993): "Star Trek: The Next Generation – Descent"

[78] Schrage, Michael / Schwartz, Jeff / Kiron, David / Jones, Robin / Buckley, Natasha (2020): "Opportunity Marketplaces"

held responsible for the offered content.

The development of the Digital Twin started with a digital model, created to appear like the physical original. Then both got connected with a continuous of interchange of information. Linked with an avatar, the PDT would be visible. This allows to detect subconscious behavior, and due to this, make it conscious.[79] A concept which aligns with the philosophy of transcendence.

Based on the philosopher Immanuel Kant, self-awareness (including self-confidence) is based on observation and reflection of oneself. To get to know the own self & personality, a person must construct the idea that he / she has of oneself. With this, the individual is observer and observed, subject and object. The sociologist William Bruce Cameron once said: *"Not everything that can be counted counts, and not everything that counts can be counted."* Accordingly, it can be concluded that values and attitudes count, but cannot be counted so far. A PDT may make them countable. That way, values and norms get visible, and via the PDT could be integrated into the corporate system, to measure, but also to change non-adequate subconscious behavior, or the even the other way around, positive subconscious can influence the corporate system.

The PDT takes on the role of the observer, as its first task is to logically construct a realistic virtual copy of the individual. Nevertheless, the employee also observes the twin, as he /she may access the twin, via dash-board or even

---

[79] De Kerckhove, Derrick / Saracco, Roberto (2020): "IEEE Virtual Tech Talk Personal Digital Twins"

communicate with his / her three-dimensional manifestation inside a virtual reality. Due to this, the PDT might get perceived like an existing or fictional individual. If the employees like and respect what they see, they will try to comply and follow its recommendations. In parallel, roles switches, so that the employee can observe the PDT and achieve a better self-awareness.

De Kerckhove and Saracco predict that the rise of Person Digital Twins will shift culture from "guilt" to "shame". From the internal feeling guilty, future employees may feel ashamed for the perception of their PDT. Feeling guilty is based on the understanding of having committed an offense or deviation to guideline / law, while employees may feel ashamed, as embarrassed of their virtual twin.

The moment potential new employees apply for a position, companies often invite them to conduct a personality test. If not then, such often get done in later team-building events. A known concept is for example, the DISC assessment. The tool-kit is based the psychologist William Moulton Marston, who identified four difference personality traits: dominance, inducement, submission and compliance.[80] Later the in 1965, Peter Merenda and Walter Clarke published their essay *"Self-description and personality measurement"* in the Journal of Clinical Psychology, where they present the an updated DISC self-assessment with the factors: dominance, influence, steadiness and conscientiousness.[81]

---

[80] Marston, William Moulton (1928): "Emotions of Normal People"

[81] Merenda, Peter F. / Clarke, Walter V. (1965): "Self description and

Equipped with an Artificial Intelligence and via smart-phone, -watch or other wearables, the PDT connects continuously with the individual. Due to this, it monitors and records conscious and subconscious behavior. In opposite to the word "twin", physical ideas lose their meanings in the virtual world. Like the manufacturing industry, individuals will not have one PDT, but various ones. Depending on which direction the development will go, people might have one holistic PDT, a private one, a scholar one, or also a corporate one. Even if all twins are related to the individual, the ownership may vary.

Today employees receive a company laptop and smart-phone. In future, a PDT may be added to the list. Aligned with the idea, the human and AI collaborate as team, the PDT (beta) analyzes the situation and suggest "its" human (alpha) an adequate action. This could be based on a group of individuals, for example "5 out of 6 Compliance Officers decided to do this in a comparable situation", but also based on earlier observed behavior of the individual, like "in 23 out of 30 comparable situations, you decided that way."

This supports the decision-making and makes the single employee more transparent, what rises new legal, but also ethical questions.

- Ownership: A PDT can learn to behave and decide like its owner. This means, based on identified patterns (scenario), it could execute a similar "behavioral script" like the employee would do. As

---

personality measurement"

conclusion, after the algorithm is efficiently trained, it may substitute the original employee if he/she retires or even earlier. This can support in the transition phase, as the PDT can train the successor, but also that the PDT directly (at least partly) replaces the human employee.

- Antitrust: If employees would switch between different competitors, in an extreme case, this may lead to the effect that all virtual employees act the same and due to this, companies act like a monopoly or oligopoly.

- Management: Making employee behavior and related results transparent, it enables the automation of the management function. Employees which not comply with a certain level of positive results, deviate laws & corporate regulations, or overstep agreed risk levels (as risk-appetite is management decision), could (semi-) automatic dismissed from the company.

Employee and PDT may act like a self-fulfilling prophecy. If he / she perceives his / her PDT as a transparent and respected character, on a higher grade he / she will take accept the recommendations from the twin. This will be observed, so that it fosters the positive presentation of the PDT. This effect may tempt companies to let employees not to see and interact with their direct PDT, but let them perceive a better and more positive version of themselves. This to raise the opportunity to use the PDT as micro influencer towards the employee.

Deming underlined the importance of having the theory in a letter to fellow statistician Ronald D. Moen, where he classified the known "Plan-Do-Check-Act"-circle (PDCA, comparable to a statistical relation between input and output) as "corruption".[82] In opposite to this he developed, or at least contributed to, the "Plan-Do-Study-Act"-system (PDSA, comparable to a logical relation).[83] Related to the concept of the PDT, it supports the employees to monitor its own behavior and check that it complies with the requirements of the tasks. Going beyond, as the twin makes behavior visible, employees can use this information to reflect what they have, why, and what in future they might do instead.

The corporate PDT is a company tool, so its first obligation is with the corporation, not its physical counter-part. If not limited by local data privacy law, the HR can use the PDT to predict the employee's behavior, not only based on knowledge and experience, but also observed behavior and concluded underlying attitudes. This can include that the algorithm could predict in which potential scenarios the employee would violate laws and guidelines.[84]

Especially in global or local companies with various work locations, the Compliance Officer can use the PDT as intermediate in the communication with the employee. The

---

[82] Deming W. Edwards (1990): "Personal letter to Ronald D. Moen"

[83] Moen, Ronald D. / Norman, Clifford L. (2010): "circling back"

[84] Henz, Patrick (2019): "Tomorrow's Business Ethics – Philip K. Dick vs. W. Edwards Deming"

PDT has access to the various Compliance topics and workshops. If due to his / her tasks the employee may require additional training, the PDT can alert the employee and automatically lead him / her to the online training or information, or schedule a meeting with the Compliance Officer.

Human managers today do career planning together with their HR partner. In future, the combination of the employee's knowledge, certifications, observed behavior, character profile and job profile may predict the development based on algorithm, not only the career, but also in which scenarios the employee is on risk to violate regulations and laws.

Of course, such development strongly depends on still-to-come laws regarding data privacy and retirements. Imperative is furthermore a strong cyber-protection to not risk the employees' trust into the corporate system. In this phase the PDT starts to overlap with the human employee, leading to the next step, that the PDT stays, while the original human retires. Aligned with Deming, the PDT does not connect only horizontally with the employee, but connects back to the past. Accordingly, it documents the whole timeframe the employee was active for the company. If can portray the employee at any given time.

In a not-to-soon future, employees may start in a company, receiving their corporate IT-tools, including a new PDT, pre-loaded with the employee's curriculum and the conclusions from the recruitment test (for example DISC). From this moment on, the twin accompanies the employee, observes and learns. For white-collar positions, this enables the PDT to partly take-over decision making from the employee and continue working in his / her absence, including weekends and holidays. As labor law may confirm that business decisions are company property, the PDT may stay active even if the employee retires or switches the company.

Similar cases already exist. The 2016 movie "Rogue One: A Star Wars Story"[85] is in the franchise' time-line shortly before the 1977 "Star Wars: Episode IV – A New Hope".[86] This made it necessary to bring back the character of Grand Moff Tarkin, originally interpreted by the charismatic British actor Peter Cushing (1913 – 1994). Disney decided against the option to let another actor play this role, but instead used Cushing's earlier performance, digitalized him and let a digital twin act in the movie. Important, this virtual manifestation not only included the outer appearance, but also his way of acting. The results of his professional analysis of this role. As Disney (via Lucasfilm) owns the original copyrights, it may argue that they have right to do so. Nevertheless, the company not relied on a potential court-decision, but instead negotiated with his descendants. The actors' union SAG-AFTRA confirmed the last as the adequate handling: *"Using a digital or virtual re-creation of a performer, deceased or living, in a film, television show, video game, or any other audio-visual work, requires, at minimum, prior consent of the performer or the performers' beneficiaries. The issue for us is*

---

[85] Edwards, Gareth (2016): "Rogue One: A Star Wars Story"

[86] Lucas, George (1977): "Star Wars: Episode IV – A New Hope"

straightforward and clear: The use of performers' work in this manner has obvious economic value and should be treated accordingly." The statement represents the opinion of the union, and so far, had not been challenged by court.[87]

As employees, individuals take on different roles and act accordingly. Professor Philip Zimbardo famously confirmed this with the "Stanford Prison Experiment".[88] Their performance has an economic value, as described by the union.

Return to the DIKW hierarchy including data, information, knowledge and wisdom, we can conclude that a Personal Digital Twin is on the third or even fourth level, as at least it includes the employee's knowledge. If this is aligned with a stronger AI, the knowledge may evolve to wisdom recommending the adequate actions for the company's benefit. Typically, data and information are subject to privacy agreements. Deming defined: *"Without data, you're just another person with an opinion."* With this thought, we can conclude that if we take away the data and information from the PDT, its knowledge would also be gone, as the algorithm could not decide due to missing data. This as the Artificial Intelligence not achieves classic knowledge, but decides on stored data and its statistical relations (information). With continues Machine Learning, the algorithm may foster the learned conclusions (statistical relations), or slightly change them.

---

[87] Lincoln, Kevin (2016): "How Did *Rogue One* Legally Re-Create the Late Peter Cushing?"

[88] Zimbardo, Philip G. (1971): "The power and pathology of imprisonment"

This in opposite to the human employee. Even if the brain is a super-computer, it does not offer the option to erase restricted information for the case that an employee leaves a company. Data itself may not be remembered, but information yes. After a while, also the information may blur, nevertheless the related knowledge still be remembered for a longer time. As past data and information are not available, incl. newer data and information not included, the knowledge turns into opinion.

In opposite to Machine Learning, humans can form theories without underlying data. Such logical opinions stay relevant until data can be collected to confirm or disconfirm the theory. Abstract information does not automatically open a road to gain knowledge. For example, the contemplation of an abstract art work may not offer details about the desired interpretation, nevertheless it may inspire the observer to complete new ideas, including for work. A point for art at the workplace.

Opinions may stay valid, if it is based on enough experience. Due to this, even without access to data, it may create wisdom, to be used for prediction. A reason companies are interested hiring employees from its competitors and other industries.

As often, the options are between black and white. In the case of retirement, the company may take the decision, to not directly let the PDT be active inside the organization, but instead dissolve it and enter its data into a collective digital twin, including all retired employees, or even a collective of all active and retired employees. Doing so, the data from the particular PDT could get weighted and marked using blockchain technology. That way, the company's management could decide to ask the whole collective digital twin for a recommendation, or let it use only a collection of former employees, for example, a weighted opinion from all former CEOs.

A futuristic idea, but nothing completely new, as also without Artificial Intelligence parts of employees' knowledge, ideas and values stay active. We can assume that an entrepreneur has neither a book of internal norms & regulations, nor a written code of conduct with defined corporate values. In the beginning of a company, there are typically only a handful of employees. Due to this, such documents are not been necessary. Everyone has direct contact with the boss, and understand what is expected from the employees. With business success come rising workload and number of employees. The founder does not have time anymore to explain each employee what to do, so it becomes necessary to write work-manuals. Furthermore, labor-laws and unions require to define workers' rights and requirements, tax laws require to establish efficient accounting, and so on. To ensure that everybody knows and follows the original vision, it is imperative to define values as corporate values. The company's Code of Conduct defines the various norms and expected behavior. All other internal regulations base on the CoC. The various documents are based on the founder and represent his / her values, attitudes, experience and knowledge. Despite the founder, each employee shapes the organization. Key-employees are responsible to define new corporate regulations, processes, routines, and norms, even may update the Code of Conduct from time to time. Shaping the processes and regulations, even updating the CoC from time-to-time, means changing the corporate system. Similar to the human backbone, the knowledge of former employees stays subconsciously active inside the company.

As discussed earlier in the book, the founder has particular importance for the company, as his or her visions survived inside the corporate values, Code of Conduct or other regulations & structures. If available, the corporate museum is a priceless source to discover biographies, speeches, decisions and other information linking directly to the founder. Using this data, it is possible to create a PDT of the founder, which might be used as counselor. Deming concluded that new knowledge must come from the outside of the organization. On the other hand, a known risk for companies is that knowledge is available at one part, but not in other ones. In addition, knowledge is often not documented and protected, so that it cannot only leave the organization, but also get lost in the case of retirements. Especially in times, where parts of the workforce get replaced by machines and algorithms, companies must ensure that human knowledge stays inside the organization. Besides sophisticated concepts as the PDT, this can be reached with the establishment of knowledge bases. For various topics, YouTube became such, as users not only look for entertainment, but also access the platform for cooking recipes or to learn how to repair a washing-machine. As every smart-phone and laptop include a camera and recording-function, companies can create similar short-videos to explain basic and sophisticated topics. This could be used in combination with presenting PowerPoint-slides.

That way the slides include the data & information, and the employee's explanation provides the knowledge. Such a knowledge base can be accessed by the employees, depending the security-level also with restrictions. If we add the founder's PDT, that way the present dots interlink into the past to keep, like the concept of Renaissance, knowledge alive. Organizations are in a constant flow, as employees are changing, but also ecosystems. A PDT cannot make a dot to endure, but establishes a similar one. Even more, if the company does not have a classic founder, as for example, it is the result of merger or outsourcing; or it is a quite recent organization, it is possible to create a fictive history. This can be done, to link the company's vision to a historic event or person. In the case of the inventor Nikola Tesla, even two companies followed this strategy. Elon Musk's "Tesla, Inc." and the lesser known "Nikola Motor Company".

1.5.5 Compliance New Defined

"Disruption" is in fashion today, to stop the current and give opportunity for the new. Disruption does not automatically mean that something will be implemented, but that a break can be used to reflect about the status quo and potential alternatives. A new decision-making process chooses between continuing on the known path or change to a new one.

For an individual, regular disruptions are required to avoid a "tunnel vision" and related behavior risks. In our modern times it gets increasingly complicated to get a break, as thanks to connected smart devices employees read and answer their emails not only inside their regular working hours, but also before and after, including on week-ends and holidays. Even the classic TV-evening does not give the required escape, as tablet and smart phones became a regular "second screen" to switch the eyes between TV and computer.

Important possibilities for disruption are the employee's holidays or also business travels. "Traveling educates" is not only a phrase, but new locations and meeting other people are always a source of inspiration. The individual connects the new impression with his or her actual life and tasks. After the time off, such new ideas can make the person re-think his or her tasks and, hopefully, make such more effective.

The company's HR department shall ensure that employees take their annual holidays, and furthermore that over-time gets limited. Employees with a "private life" receive input from different settings, as they interconnect with more dots. Inspirations and fresh ideas get back to the company and due to this, the employee gets more valuable for the organization. Bill Gates understood this relation and once said: *"I choose a lazy person to do a hard job. Because a lazy person will find an easy way to do it."* He formulated it provocative, because being outside the office does not mean being lazy, as leisure time can be used actively.

Especially today, where jobs get automatized by robots and AI, the company shall be aware that on positions where we need human employees, they treat them as such and not similar to machines. If not, humans are vulnerable for failures and errors. Humans treated as humans, develop the skills to protect themselves against negative psychological biases.

Disruption is relevant for all corporate functions. The Compliance department is still a relative new function, implemented as reaction to big corporate scandals or new legal requirements. It had been added to already existing organizational functions. Now it is a good time to take a break and analyze if this setup is the best fit, or if we want to have something else.

William Edwards Deming started as an electrical engineer who specialized later in mathematical physics, before he became a management consultant. Based on his background he took a different view on organizational structures and elaborated his *"System of Profound Knowledge"*, including the four pillars:

- Appreciation for a system
- Knowledge about variation
- Theory of Knowledge
- Psychology[89]

To ensure an efficient change management, Deming first had to convince his clients that his systematical approach had been adequate and brought a fresh insight. He presented all different company functions from procurement to sales as one big system, where the different parts interact with each other, including with external stakeholders. Deming's clients understood and appreciated this systematical approach. After this, he could analyze the different available options and how the variation of decisions could lead to higher or lower efficiency level of the whole system. This required expert knowledge to forecast the outcome. The idea was to use cognitive learning instead a simple trail-and-error-approach. Based on his research, Deming concluded that the employees are part of the system, but playing an outstanding role.

In his later role as business consultant for Toyota he implemented this concept in 2001, known as *"The Toyota Way"*. The two pillars included "Continuous Improvement" and "Respect for People". This is not only a symbiosis of US and Japanese philosophy, but can be identified in all time and cultures as base for business success. Already decades earlier Enzo Ferrari defined the company's output as result

---

[89] W. Edwards Deming (1986): "Out of the Crisis"

of effective teamwork: *"What we do here is elite work."*[90]

Based on his psychological knowledge, Deming recognized that a non-efficient infrastructure, a bureaucratic burden, has a negative impact on the employees. Taking Donald Cressey's Fraud Triangle[91] into consideration, bureaucracy is a temptation to bypass it, especially if its benefit is not understandable. Due to this, the organizational setup (physical location, tools, processes, guidelines, company values) must be created to support the employees and not the other way around. This philosophy is aligned with the concept of Industry 4.0, where automatization adapts to the user and not the human employee to the machines, as still in Industry 3.0

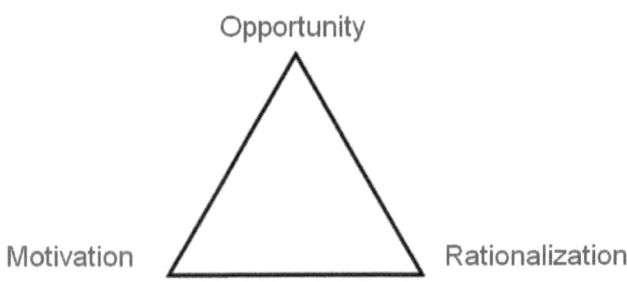

Based on a systematical approach, what triggers compliance with internal guidelines and external laws? *"Information"*. Information what is the adequate behavior, what is the

---

[90] Henz, Patrick (2017): "Business Philosophy according to Enzo Ferrari"

[91] Crassey, David (1973): "Other People's Money: A Study in the Social Psychology of Embezzlement"

content of the relevant guidelines and what is the potential result of the behavior (likelihood and impact, including for "getting caught with violation a law of guideline"). The individual must understand the cost of corruption, before he or she can develop empathy for the victims. The Ethics & Compliance Officer must reduce the costs to gain information, for example by being close to the business.

Information is the critical resource for businesses and organizations, as they require access and ownership of such. Information is mandatory for successful companies and its value is on the raise. It is no surprise that information becomes even jewelry. The US Rosetta Project seeks via crowd-funding to finance its first prototype of a long-term archive. The only three-inch diameter nickel disk should store 14,000 pages of information. Like the famous Rosetta Stone, it should include over 1,000 languages to store them for the next thousands of years. The production of numerous disks should ensure that at least a few of them survive the centuries.[92] The small size makes the Rosetta Disk an ideal object to create necklace or other piece of art or jewelry.[93] Another example is "FrontRow" from Uniquiti Labs, a camera for livestreams in the form of a necklace. Thanks to its operational system, the device can send the videos automatically to platforms like Facebook or a video-blog.[94]

---

[92] The Rosetta Project (fetched 30.06.2020)

[93] Sayej, Nadja (2017): "This Old School Wearable Puts a Thousand Languages Around Your Neck"

[94] Lazzaro, Sage (2017): "Look, no hands! $399 camera necklace lets you livestream videos directly to Facebook, Instagram, and YouTube without

The problem with information is not only a potential missing access to it, also the opposite: the overflow caused by numerous news portals and social platforms makes it impossible for humans to timely analyze information. Specialized providers and AI software may get used to summarize the daily articles and decide which are relevant and which not. As perceptional biases always exist, it is the question, how reliable are such services, especially if a computer should decide what is relevant for humans.[95] Trust is needed, especially if the success of the company depends on this information. Such providers must be auditable.

Reality is not the same for people, in fact, everyone builds its own reality, based on information and the perception of information. In George Orwell's classic "1984" the characters Winston and O'Brien discussed if the past exists. In the beginning of the dialogue it is clear: *"In records. It is written down."*[96] A logical definition, as we think to know our past, as it is documented in history books. Sometimes a false perceived safety, as books only represent the actual status of history. Theories exist until they get dis-confirmed. History books must be rewritten, when archeologists find new clues and evidence. The more a thesis gets communicated, the more believable it sounds. Especially when it comes from different sources, which gets perceived as independent. This

lifting a finger"

[95] Knight, Will (2017): "An Algorithm Summarizes Lengthy Text Surprisingly Well"

[96] Orwell, George (1949): "1984"

applies for correct and false information. Relevant is that new information gets perceived based on the already existing experience. Like using glasses, personal believes frame the perception of new information. It is a logical conclusion for Orwell's character: *"reality is not external and only exists in the human mind, and nowhere else."*[97] Each new information gets perceived through the glasses of existing information. Furthermore, with this it changes slowly the individual's inner reality. If information gets erased from books, websites, and other alternative information communicated, the original reality will become unreal for the perceiver; later forgotten and replaced by the new message. In other words, it is *"the abolition of the past".*[98] This effect can be used for the good and bad. If a corporation wants to implement a relevant change, it should work with repeated messages to present a vision of the new reality. With the repeating, employees will perceive it as relevant and the existing perceived reality slowly gets understood as a status which must be changed.

Joshua Hartshorne suggested to think about the way that language frames thoughts: *"words are very handy mnemonics. We may not remember what seventeen spools looks like, but we can remember the word seventeen."*[99] The English language distinguishes between "accountability" and "responsibility":

---

[97] Orwell, George (1949): "1984"

[98] Mohomed, Carimo (2011): "The abolition of the Past: History in George Orwell's 1984"

[99] Hartshorne, Joshua (2009): "Does Language Shape What We Think?"

- Accountability: *"In ethics and governance, accountability is answerability, blameworthiness, liability, and the expectation of account-giving."*[100]

- Responsibility: *"Responsibility may refer to: being in charge, being the owner of task or event."*[101]

"Accountability" is stronger than "responsibility", as it includes the individual's perception of ownership.[102] Roman languages, however, do not define this difference. Less precise they translate "accountability" as the weaker "responsibility" (Italian: "responsabilità", Portuguese: "responsabilidade", Spanish: "responsabilidad"). This indicates a risk that target groups from these countries are less familiar with the concept of "accountability". For Ethics & Compliance-communication and -workshops this means that it must be ensured that texts with the two words get adequately translated, and if a training speaks about responsibility and / or accountability, the facilitator has to explain the specific differences.

Besides the language barrier, chat-bots infuse new risks into the transportation of information. In- and outside the corporation the creation and communication of information gets automated. In general, this supports a higher level of quality, as even specialized documents and articles get sent to the right target group. But again, as all connected software, they are vulnerable against hacker-

---

[100] Diffen (fetched 16.11.2017): "Accountability vs. Responsibility"

[101] Diffen (fetched 16.11.2017): "Accountability vs. Responsibility"

[102] YouTube (2009): "Responsibility vs Accountability"

attacks, biases and viruses. If this is the case, they can sabotage the information-flow by shutting down the service or the creation and transportation of wrong information.

Even if reality only exists inside the individual, organizations must ensure that at least these realities get similar. This can get reached by using adequate ("real") information from "objective" sources. The better the input of information, the better also the results of the decision-making process. This applies for human and artificial intelligence.

Based on this idea, Compliance hast to ensure transparency and minimize the costs to gain reliable information. Raising levels of misinformation (including perceptional bias) are a Compliance risk, as it leads to non-adequate behavior.

If we set the focus on "information", it is logical that the Compliance department is not only responsible for human employees, but also to foster data privacy and cybersecurity. Adequate behavior requires transparent information, as behavior is based on information. This is true for human employees and Artificial Intelligence. Amazon CEO Jeff Bezos said in 2017 that A.I. is in its golden age. The first companies already implemented such intelligent software and all others will follow in the next months and years. Human employees and AI have both to follow the rules and guidelines. Compliance is an established function to do this for humans, so it is a natural evolution that the department will take on this responsibility also for AI.

Traditional computer security has the goal to protect against autonomous attacks. Understanding how the IT protection of an organization works, most hackers identified the human employee as the weak brick inside the firewall. As result, most of today's cyberattacks are based on cognitive hacking. This strategy is dangerous, as the hackers not only know how the computer works, but also how the brain does. The attacks take advantage of the different psychological biases, as for example obedience to authority or on the other hand the wish to help people in need. Similar to situations in the "real world", such cognitive hacks can lead to "ethical blindness" and related non-adequate behavior, such as violating of guidelines and corruption. Just as a Trojan Virus, the misinformation gets into the human brain and delude the individual a different reality to trigger a non-adequate behavior.

At the end is the human brain nothing else a super-computer and the protection of both, human and computer, is similar. Inspired by the "Framework of Improving Critical Infrastructure Cybersecurity", an Integrity Program can be described with Identify, Protect, Detect, Respond and Recover.[103]

Even if the focus of the Integrity of Information (IoI)-program would be on "Protect", the heart is on "Detect". Efficient controls not only ensure transparency, and is a required process to win information, but furthermore create respect for the Integrity Officer (IO). To ensure this, the

---

[103] National Institute of Standards and Technology (2014): "Framework for Improving Critical Infrastructure Cybersecurity"

processes and controls shall be only as bureaucratic as required to be as strong as possible. To reach this, a continuous review of its guidelines, tools and controls is part of the "Protect"-pillar. As even the strongest control system cannot detect every violation on time, an anonymous whistleblower hotline is a mandatory add-on and of course, its effective, control. If required, investigations must gather needed information.

The day-by-day IoI-tasks are related to "Protect" and minimize potential findings in the third pillar. The IO can reach this with being near to the business and organize relevant trainings and workshops with the employees. In these events, required information gets interchanged so that both sides understand the other. The information access is relevant inside the organization, so cannot be reduced to personal meetings, as the chance for such a limited. The classic additional option is one-way communication, such as flyers, posters or even newsletters. Artificial Intelligence is offering new ways. Chat-bots can provide a first service level. The employee has the possibility to get answers to his or her frequent levels, even without that the IO gets aware of this missing of knowledge. An important point for cultures, where the "loss of the face" is a relevant factor.

Information is the base of decisions and the company's most important asset. Non-complete or even altered information lead to wrong decisions, even violation of law and guidelines.

Based on this philosophy, Compliance is a service department and friendliness necessary. But to earn respect, this is not enough, Compliance must prove that they are able to ensure guidelines and if necessary, execute adequate disciplinary sanctions. As Al Capone once said: *"Don't mistake my kindness for weakness."* If Compliance has this ability to implement such sanctions, employees understand that nobody is above the company guidelines and may overcome the fear to report potential deviations. The absence of impunity motivates employees to play by the rules and demand this from their colleagues, but also management.

The Integrity of Information system includes five pillars, designed around their central one "Detect".

- Identify: Not only each company, but each location and department is different. A regular Integrity Risk Assessment is mandatory to efficiently protect the organization. It identifies the risk factors and the required follow-up actions.

- Protect: If the organization is not in actual problems the focus shall be to stay in this situation. Transparency of information shall be fostered, employees receive the information they need based on their job position. Tailor-made communication avoids an information-overflow and so the situation that the individual rejects information or would not be able to perceive it.

- Detect: The traditional heart of the integrity system. The controls should not only detect direct violations, but in general create transparency if the processes are effective, including the preventive measures.

- Respond: "Tone from the Top" is the base for integrity, as nobody can be above the internal guidelines. Due to this, if a violation gets detected, the response must be adequate, related to the action and not the level of the person.

- Recover: Violations affect the corporate culture up to damaging reputation and causing financial damage. Even the best integrity system cannot guarantee 100% protection, so different scripts must be prepared how to react in a potential corruption case to limit the reputational damage and finally recover integrity.

As Agent Smith said in the Matrix: *"Never send a human to do a machine's job."*[104] Under ideal conditions, human employees can decide on the same quality level as AI. But in opposite to machines, they do not consistently work at their highest levels, but are influenced by mood, distraction, health and other factors. AI is superior for rule-based tasks. The human strength is creativity and the flexibility to adapt and react to different scenarios. To strengthen the human workforce, the company must treat them as such. Tasks which are possible to delegate to machines. Compliance messages should inspire and make people think. Humans remember more efficiently, if the information is the result of a thinking-process. Based on this, the Compliance idea should not make it too easy for the employee, but provoke them to think, how to understand it. For example, if an

---

[104] The Wachowskis (1999): "The Matrix"

employee has a question for the Compliance Officer, he or she should not directly answer, but send the question back to the employee to solve it on his or her own. As Compliance in most cases is based on common sense, the answer will be correct. The Compliance Officer can confirm this or if required, explain the employee where he or she went wrong.

The learning theory is based on learnt situations, which triggers to execute a learnt behavior, as this leads with a high possibility to a motivator, which satisfies the need. For example, a sales employee needs to pay its open bills, and bribes a procurement person of the client organization. With this he reaches a higher bonus to pay the personal bills. This situation not only applies for objective needs, but also subjective temptations, as the more expensive car or luxury vacations. If the used behavior leads to regular success, the employee will most probably continue with it. Further this extrinsic motivation gets replaced by an intrinsic one. The external motivator is not required anymore to trigger the corrupt behavior. The employee enjoys the flow-experience of bypassing internal process and external laws. Thanks to the ignoring of rules, life gets easier for him or her, a certain feeling of liberty or even superiority gets perceived. As the external amplifier is not required, the corrupt behavior gets shown also in situations with an only minimal benefit. This explains why repeatedly high-level employees get caught in small crimes, where the risk of jeopardizing a long business career does not stand in any relation to the potential benefit of violating internal guidelines. Depending on the individual character and the case where such behavior not got caught & sanctioned in the past, employees may underestimate the risk of getting caught. This is an opportunity for the Compliance system, as suspicious behavior can get caught in the regular random samples to control the approval- and control-processes, as for example in sponsoring and donation or the travel expenses. Mafia gangster Al Capone was imprisoned in 1931, not for murder, money-laundry, kidnapping or similar, but tax evasion. First, he spent his time in the Federal Prison of Atlanta, before he got transferred to Alcatraz, the prison island in the Bay of San Francisco. 1939 he could leave based on his good behavior.[105]

Alcatraz, San Francisco

To avoid that a flow-experience even starts, the organization must establish a clear "0 tolerance"-culture. This not only regarding potential violations of Compliance processes, but all guidelines.

If now we take a moment of disruption, we may conclude that the actual Compliance setup is understandable based on history, as many corporations implemented it to manage the risk coming from existing anti-corruption laws or even as

---

[105] Henz, Patrick (2019): "Compliance is a Race Car."

answer to an actual case.

The authors Nicolas Racz, Edgar Weippl and Andreas Seufert defined a different model, an integrated vision of Governance, Risk and Compliance (GRC). A holistic approach, where the three functions enter their specific responsibilities:[106]

- Governance ensures that the company has the required guidelines and tools implemented. They must be as strong as necessary to answer to a given risk or opportunity, but on the other hand as non-bureaucratic as possible. The processes must be transparent, and willingly violations sanctioned. Of course, processes must be adequately communicated. This not only includes the elaboration of the guideline itself, but also communication and training. The process-owner must be aware of his or her responsibility to foster compliance with the document.

- Risk: Guidelines and processes have no self-purpose, but are related to specific risks and opportunities. If such not exist (anymore), there is no reason for a guideline to carry on. It is management's decision, how high the organization's appetite for risk is. This based on its oversight of adequate information. Guidelines document this decision, what concludes employees' duty to comply.

---

[106] Racz, Niclas / Weippl, Edgar / Seufert, Andreas (2010): "A Frame of Reference for Research of Integrated Governance, Risk and Compliance (GRC)"

- In opposite to Governance, where the focus is to comply with adequate internal guidelines, Compliance concentrates on external laws, especially based on antitrust, anti-corruption and money-laundry.

The three areas create a triangle, which includes strategy, processes, people and technology. The last two are especially in the process of disruption. For example, the values and attitudes of Generation Y and Z have become a bigger part of today's workforce. On the technology side, Industry 4.0 and Artificial Intelligence offer fascinating opportunities, but also new risks. Machines may work more effectively than humans, but they also suffer from biases and data protection risks. Today people and technologies change processes and strategies. The model does not mean that GRC is responsible for these four areas, but GRC must interact with their respective owners.

The 2016 movie "Arrival"[107] (based on the 1998 short story "The Story of Life" by Ted Chiang[108]) presented twelve UFOs arriving on Earth. The alien lifeforms, the "Heptapods", had a different kind of communication, circle-like expressions, with no end and no beginning. This as the culture existed outside a linear timeline. Past, present and future had been known, as they existed in parallel. Such an understanding would mean that framing effects do not exist, as everything gets perceived the same time. For the

---

[107] Villeneuve, Denis (2016): "Arrival"

[108] Chiang, Ted (1998): "The Story of Life"

GRC triangle this would be for benefit, as the function has the temptation to be interpreted based from which angle you perceive it. When GRC evolves from Risk Management, often it will be perceived as an extended version from such. Similar when it starts from the Governance function. For a Compliance Officer taking on the GRC role, it might be different, as Compliance normally works with values and guidelines, already has inside its core function a holistic approach, so would be open to the additional tasks. If GRC gets implemented into a completely new company, the starting point would be the risk assessment. Here the risks & opportunities get identified and top management must decide which level of risk appetite the new-born organization shall live out. If GRC gets introduced into an existing company, most properly risk management, governance and compliance already exist. Like the Heptapods' language, the three points create a triangle, no beginning no end. The new responsible must define the new function or department, addressing all three angles in parallel.

With ensuring clear structures inside an organization, GRC ensures understandable rules. It protects the employees, if they play inside these rules. Employer and employee trust each other, what both understand as sign of mutable respect.

1.6 Afterglow

Implementing system-thinking into the Ethics & Compliance-function means to add a third dimension to Deming's concept of the interconnected organization: time. Today's companies can efficiently link back to its founder, to let it guide by his / her visions and values. Furthermore, a sustainable strategy connects to an envisioned point in the future:

Values + Compliance + Strategy = Sustainability

To ensure that the company stays inside legal boundaries, the Compliance department must have access to the company's strategy to analyze, if the aimed goal is ethical and reachable. If this is understood, Compliance can be the trusted partner to accompany the business colleagues to reach this vision.

The Good System

"COMPLIANCE IS A RACE CAR."

"Compliance is a Race Car.", Patrick Henz, 2019, 3. edition, 188 pages

ISBN-10: 1545157634, ISBN-13: 978-1545157633

The idea of this book is to go further than being a manual for Compliance, as it should work on different levels. Newcomers and experts can learn about the different parts of an effective Ethics & Compliance program. The toolbox questions support the reader to understand if the own program is adequate or requires optimization. Furthermore, the book demonstrates that all parts of the program interact with each other, and the whole is more than the pure addition of the single items.

The book invites the reader to a time travel, as it goes to the past to analyze what Compliance can learn from the structures of a traditional Mafia organization (always keeping in mind that Compliance and Mafia stand on opposite sides). Then it brings us back to the creation of a successful race car, to blast off and investigate the near future to present the new challenges based on robotics and Artificial Intelligence.

The different trips not only underline that "travelling educates" and due to this, Compliance is not a function to stay behind a desk, but furthermore Ethics & Compliance is a task, which can be interpreted based on the own character and offers the required space and flexibility to climb up Maslow's Pyramids.

BUSINESS PHILOSOPHY ACCORDING TO ENZO FERRARI

"An inspiration for managers, leaders and everybody who is interested in Enzo Ferrari's life."

Born 1898 in the Northern-Italian city of Modena, Enzo Ferrari lived his dream and founded the world's most famous sports car manufacturer. This book analyzes how he achieved his goals by what are considered to be modern concepts. Or were leadership theories, emotional intelligence, business ethics, client orientation and sustainability already guiding principles of business in the beginning of the last century.

In his own words, and drawing several parallels to Italian history, he thought he was living in the wrong time. But taking off Il Commendatore's sunglasses, this book presents him as a surprisingly modern leader, who, conscious or not, acted conform the latest business and leadership models, confirmed by key decisions of his company, including the racing-team.

Therefore, the book not only uses racing decisions and car development as examples, including many photos, but sets them in relation to his personal business philosophy.

7. edition, 370 pages, ISBN-10: 1548099074, ISBN-13: 978-1548099077

2 BIBILOGRAPHY

- Ackoff, Russell Lincoln (1989): "From Data to Wisdom"
- Asch, Salomon E.: (1951): "Effects of group pressure on the modification and distortion of judgments."
- BusinessDictionary (fetched 04.04.2020): "contract": http://www.businessdictionary.com/definition/contract.html#:~:t ext=A%20voluntary%2C%20deliberate%2C%20and%20legally,sale %20or%20lease%2C%20or%20tenancy.
- Chiang, Ted (1998): "The Story of Life"
- Cohen (1992): "Anthem"
- Crane, David (1982): "Pitfall!"
- Cressey, Donald (1973): "Other People's Money: A Study in the Social Psychology of Embezzlement"

- deGrasse Tyson, Neil (2017): "Astrophysics for People in a Hurry"
- Deming, W. Edwards (1950): "Lecture to Japanese Management"
- Deming, W. Edwards (1986): "Out of the Crisis"
- Deming W. Edwards (1990): "Personal letter to Ronald D. Moen"
- Deming, W. Edwards (1993): "The New Economics for Industry, Governance, Education"
- Dick, Philip K. (1968): "Do Androids dream of Electric Sheep?"
- Dick, Philip K. (1985): "I Hope I Shall Arrive Soon"
- Dimock, Michael (2019): "Defining generations: Where Millennials end and Generation Z begins": https://www.pewresearch.org/fact-tank/2019/01/17/where-millennials-end-and-generation-z-begins/
- Eliot, Thomas Stearns (1934): The Rock
- Frankenfield, Jake (2019): "What is a Smart Contract?": https://www.investopedia.com/terms/s/smart-contracts.asp
- Hao, Karen (2020): "Nearly half of Twitter accounts pushing to reopen America ay be bots": https://www.technologyreview.com/2020/05/21/1002105/covid-bot-twitter-accounts-push-to-reopen-america/
- Hartshorne, Joshua (2009): "Does Language Shape What We Think?": https://www.scientificamerican.com/article/does-language-shape-what/
- Henz, Patrick (2017): "Wirtschaftspsychologie & Compliance"
- Henz, Patrick (2019): "Business Philosophy according to Enzo Ferrari"
- Henz, Patrick (2019): "Compliance is a Race Car."

- Henz, Patrick (2019): "Tomorrow's Business Ethics – Philip K. Dick vs. W. Edwards Deming"
- Henz, Patrick (2020): "Compliance Tales & Travels"
- Homer (8th century BC): "Odyssey"
- Hunter, John (2012): "Appreciation for a System": https://blog.deming.org/2012/10/appreciation-for-a-system/
- Ironhead Studios (2020): "Concept Art": http://ironheadstudio.com/concept-art/
- Ito, Joi (2018): "Why Westerners fear Robots and the Japanese do not": https://www.wired.com/story/ideas-joi-ito-robot-overlords/
- Knight, Will (2017): "An Algorithm Summarizes Lengthy Text Surprisingly Well": https://www.technologyreview.com/2017/05/12/151734/an-algorithm-summarizes-lengthy-text-surprisingly-well/

- Kubrik, Stanley (1968): "2001: A Space Odyssey"

- Lazzaro, Sage (2017): "Look, no hands! $399 camera necklace lets you livestream videos directly to Facebook, Instagram, and YouTube without lifting a finger": https://www.dailymail.co.uk/sciencetech/article-4797486/Camera-necklace-stream-videos-directly-social-media.html

- Lovelock, James (1972): "Gaia as seen through the atmosphere"

- Lucas, George (1977): "Star Wars"

- Maslow, Abraham (1943): "A Theory of Human Motivation"

- Milgram, Stanley (1963): "Behavioral Study of Obedience"

- Miller, Larry (1983): "Enduro"

- Moen, Ronald D. / Norman, Clifford L. (2010): "circling back"

- National Institute of Standards and Technology (2014): "Framework for Improving Critical Infrastructure Cybersecurity": https://www.nist.gov/document/cybersecurity-framework-021214pdf

- NASA (2020): "The Worm is Back!"

- Nolan, Christopher (2010): "Inception"

- Omiya, Hideaki (2018): "Chowa: A Business Philosophy to Bridge a Fractured World": https://spectra.mhi.com/chowa-to-bridge-a-fractured-world

- Open Government (2019): "Electronic Transactions Act": https://open.alberta.ca/publications/e05p5

- Orwell, George (1949): "Nineteen Eighty-Four"

- Racz, Niclas / Weippl, Edgar / Seufert, Andreas (2010): "A Frame of Reference for Research of Integrated Governance, Risk and Compliance (GRC)": https://link.springer.com/chapter/10.1007/978-3-642-13241-4_11

- Rand, Ayn (1957): "Atlas Shrugged"

- Rowley, Jennifer (2007): "The wisdom hierarchy: representations of the DIKW hierarchy": https://pdfs.semanticscholar.org/088d/6a1fa59a8840ab0dff0f2e0 6d1c1fd7d4012.pdf?_ga=2.174413090.1236315546.1590100519- 1933997201.1590100519

- Rudlin, Pernille (2019): "The five elements of building trust between Japanese and European business cultures": https://www.japanintercultural.com/en/blogs/default.aspx?blogi d=2322

- Sayej, Nadja (2017): "This Old School Wearable Puts a Thousand Languages Around Your Neck": https://www.vice.com/en_us/article/qvdgn7/this-old-school-wearable-puts-a-thousand-languages-around-your-neck

- Schrage, Michael / Schwartz, Jeff / Kiron, David / Jones, Robin / Buckley, Natasha (2020): "Opportunity Marketplaces": http://mitsmr.com/2BR7i5V

- Scott, Ridley (1982): "Blade Runner"

- Serpa, Alexandre C. (2020): "Compliance Board Games":

https://ethicsplayground.wordpress.com/2020/02/06/compliance-board-games/

- Smith, Lacey (2018): "This tricked-out SpaceX helmet is nearly all 3D printed": https://mashable.com/video/spacex-helmet-3d-printed/

- Stanford University (fetched 30.06.2020): "Stanford Persuasive Tech Lab": https://captology.stanford.edu/go/welcome?from=

- Szabo, Nick (1994): "Smart Contracts"

- The DESIGN MUSEUM (2019): "Ferrari: Under the Skin": https://designmuseum.org/exhibitions/ferrari-under-the-skin

- The Rosetta Project (fetched 30.06.2020): https://rosettaproject.org/

- The United States Department of Justice (1977): "Foreign Corrupt Practices Act": https://www.justice.gov/criminal-fraud/foreign-corrupt-practices-act

- The Wachowskis (1999): "The Matrix"

- UK Legislation (2015): "Modern Slavery Act 2015": http://www.legislation.gov.uk/ukpga/2015/30/contents/enacted

- Villeneuve, Denis (2016): "Arrival"

- Werber, Cassie (2016): „"There is a crack in everything, that's how the light gets in": The story of Leonard Cohen's "Anthem"": https://qz.com/835076/leonard-cohens-anthem-the-story-of-the-line-there-is-a-crack-in-everything-thats-how-the-light-gets-in/

- Yeaworth, Irvin (1958): "The Blob"

- Zimbardo, Philip G. (1971): "The power and pathology of imprisonment"

The Good System

3 ABOUT THE AUTHOR

Patrick Henz started his career in Corporate Information and Compliance at the end of 2007, when he was responsible for the implementation of an Anti-Corruption program in Mexico and several Central American and Caribbean countries. Together with these tasks, he gained valuable insights into global Compliance programs, with a focus on Latin America. Since 2009 in his role as Compliance Officer he is responsible for an effective Compliance program; based on identification, protection, detection, response & recovery and combined with integrity, respect, passion & sustainability. With these means, he defines Compliance as pro-active function, being perceived as guardian, expert and facilitator. The focus is on information to ensure adequate behavior, not only of the human employee, but Artificial Intelligence included.

This includes the regular planning and execution of Compliance Risk Assessments and further global reviews. According an effective sustainability strategy, where Compliance plays a key role, he actively promotes this idea at university workshops and conferences (including the ACI Compliance Boot-Camp 2013, '15 and '17 in Houston). In so doing he became two times President of Honor of Marcus Evans' Latin-American Corporate Compliance Conference 2011 and '12 in Mexico City, panelist at The Economist's Mexico Summit 2015 and co-founder of the Ethics & Compliance Forum Mexico, including editor and co-author of the Ethics & Compliance Manual, published in April 2014.

Since 2013 he lives and works in Atlanta, USA